Martha F Sesselberg

In Amazon land; adaptations from Brazilian writers

With original selections

Martha F Sesselberg

In Amazon land; adaptations from Brazilian writers
With original selections

ISBN/EAN: 9783337056865

Printed in Europe, USA, Canada, Australia, Japan

Cover: Foto ©Andreas Hilbeck / pixelio.de

More available books at **www.hansebooks.com**

In Amazon Land

Adaptations from Brazilian Writers, with Original Selections

By

Martha F. Sesselberg

"Come here, come here, and dwell in forest deep!
. . . .
Come here, come here, and lie
By whispering stream,
Here health all seek, and joy,
And shun perverse annoy,
And lie 'neath bells of flowers till close of day,
And laugh—alway!"

      Barry Cornwall

G. P. PUTNAM'S SONS
NEW YORK   LONDON
27 WEST TWENTY-THIRD STREET   24 BEDFORD STREET, STRAND
The Knickerbocker Press
1893

COPYRIGHT, 1893
BY
MARTHA F. SESSELBERG

Electrotyped, Printed and Bound by
The Knickerbocker Press, New York
G. P. Putnam's Sons

IN AMAZON LAND.

Frontispiece

TO

MY PARÁ FRIENDS

BOTH BRAZILIAN AND FOREIGN, IS THIS
LITTLE BROCHURE AFFECTIONATELY
AND GRATEFULLY DEDICATED

CONTENTS.

	PAGE
A TROPIC IDYL	1
A LORELEI OF THE AMAZON	5
A TALE OF THE GREAT RIVER	9
AMAZONIAN LEGENDS	43
AMAZONIAN BELIEFS, TRADITIONS, AND SUPERSTITIONS.	53
A FISHING PARTY	67
AMAZONIAN RUBBER IN "FIRST HANDS". . .	71
SINHAZINHA !	74
AN AMAZONIAN FUNERAL . .	81
DOLCE FAR NIENTE	85
A BALL IN AMAZON LAND	87
ORCHIDS FROM A TROPICAL GARDEN .	91
[NEAR THE FOREST. A MORNING CALL. THE FESTA OF OUR LADY OF NAZARETH. A SUMMER ISLE.]	
AT REST	94

IN AMAZON LAND.

A TROPIC IDYL

MANUEL, a foppish young fellow, of whom it was difficult to decide whether more of Indian or mulatto blood rån in his veins (probably a not unequal mixture of both), was on this memorable afternoon stretched out at full length on the *girao*[1] of his father's hut.

The lingering sun tinged with gold the tall tops of the *miriti* palms, standing in stately rows along the river.

Strange birds, from branches high in air, trilled out their farewell song to day.

Saracuras, in noisy notes, burst out with their eternal "Kirikó-kirikó-kirikó-kó-kó-kó-kó!"

No other sound could be heard, save, perhaps, the croaking of frogs, or the rumbling of the great water-cart, drawn by one patient ox, and followed by the *gallego* José, who shouted out at intervals: "*Agua, agua fresca!*" (water, fresh water).

Manuel slowly rose, casting an indolent glance at his gun hanging on the *jupaty* wall, turned again in the direction of the *saracuras*, contemplated the firmament, muttering: "It is n't worth a while. I

[1] *Girao*, a rough stage raised by poles above the floor.

am*e*loyed with *saracuras*." As he uttered the last word, a tremendous crash of rockets, followed by a gunshot from the *rouqueira* (settler) roused the idle young fellow to something like animation. Pointing with his finger southward, he exclaimed: "It is there —in the house of Sr. Fabricio—there, to-night, is the *fandango*."

Donning his best cotton trousers, and shirt of scarlet hue, he leaped into his canoe, which, like some great reptile, swiftly glided over the smooth expanse of water. And at each stroke of the oar, his voice, flexible and resonant, resounded in far-repeated echoes:

> "Não tenho mêdo de onça,
> Nem das pintas que ella tem;
> Tenho medo da creoula
> Quando chega a querer bem."

Now there was in the settlement one Joanna, a handsome *cabocla* girl, with short, curly hair flying to the wind. She cared much for Manuel—but— very much—to the point that she could not bear to pass one day without seeing him. On this special occasion she had waited until the hour of nine. Then, too, fell on her ear the crash of fire-works, and the sound of the great gun of the *rouqueira*. Jumping up, an ominous light flashing in her eyes, she exclaimed in the identical words of the graceless Manuel: "It is there—in the house of Sr. Fabricio— there, to-night, is the *fandango*." A little later, a canoe, a gallant bark, freshly painted with green and yellow, followed in the wake of that other her canoe.

But it is to be noted that the *bicha* (literally "little devil") this time was not attired in her usual festive dress of gay-colored skirt, and *camisola*, adorned with "labyrinth" lace, so laboriously done over a cushion by her own hands. No, she wore the well fitting attire of her twin-brother, and in her curly head floated a scheme of revenge.

When she reached the house of Sr. Fabricio, the ball was in full tide. Instead of joining the country dance, she went about, parrying thrusts and jokes with the young men on the terrace.

Romping and laughter broke out on all sides. Many thought the new arrival a gallant young fellow.

"How plump he is," exclaimed a meagre, wizard-looking Indian, in whose veins probably flowed a drop of the anthropological blood of his ancestors.

Joanna, meanwhile, went on her way, treading with no light weight on the toes of some, who, with the instinct of nature, approached her too familiarly.

In her mouth she rakishly puffed at a great cigar of *tauary*.[1]

Just then she came face to face with Manuel, in the act of cynically entwining his arm round the waist of a coy little *roceira* (settler's daughter).

"Lend me a light, *caboclo*," she said.

He was about to do so, when a tingling blow on the cheek caused him to see more stars than are in the firmament. Snatching a knife from his belt, he was about to attack his unknown aggressor, when a

[1] A sort of tobacco made from the pith of a wild cane.

s●nd blow, shar●r than the first, brought him to the earthen floor. In his ear was whispered: "I waited for you until nine—*canalha!*"

Moments after, floated over the silent waters a canoe, and in it were two young *matutos* (rustics), cooing and billing in all the intoxicating ecstasy of happy lovers. Afar, breaking the silence of night, the echo still repeated:

> "Nào tenho mêdo de onça,
>   Nem das pintas que ella tem;
>   Tenho medo da creoula
>   Quando chega a querer bem."

A LORELEI OF THE AMAZON.

"THERE he goes!" exclaimed old Dorothea, glancing down the path by which had disppeared João, her only son, and the only prop of her isolated old age. There he goes, with a fond expression. And continued : "*Deos meo!* What can be done to dissolve this enchantment that has turned the head of my son?" Retiring to her apartment, she opened an old oratory in which were quartered several wooden saints, lighted a consecrated candle, and commenced to repeat the *Deos Padre.* Rising to her knees, she took from a calabash a few grains of *mandioca* meal, munching them meanwhile between her teeth, and turned into the same path by which had disappeared João. Mingling with the melancholy notes of crickets, as they lay hidden under the dry leaves of the *cacoal,* could be heard ever more faintly the rude refrain hummed by poor João:

"Who gives his heart away
To one he doesn't know,
For all the pain he suffers
Should suffer threefold more."[1]

The momentary tropical twilight had long since merged into darkness when the desolate old woman

[1] Quem da o seu coração
A gente que não conhece,
Por mais penas que padeca
Dobrados penas merece.

returned, her eyes swimming with tears, and in complete despair of ever being able to snatch her son from the noose of that terrible seduction into which he had fallen.

"Good-evening, Aunt Dorothea," said I, at the foot of a clump of *assai* palms.

"God give the same to you, Mr. Canuto; is it you? And wiping away with her cotton skirt two great tears, she continued. "You are still young and *bonito*" (literally pretty).

"It is like your goodness to say so, Aunt Dorethea."

"And *bonito* as my son."

"Much obliged, my good woman."

"It is nothing," said she, attempting between her tears a smile. And resumed: "My son, take care of yourself. When you go about in these latitudes, above all by canoe, don't forget your rosary."

"What is that?"

"That is what I say. Now, look at João."

"And what is the matter with João?"

"He is with his head turned."

"That is very natural. He is exactly at that age, which time brings but once, and in which the mothers say——"

"No; no, the case is other. Who said it was the sight of a petticoat? Then I would have gone to the priest; but it is—that—my son is lost." And she concluded with groans and sobs.

Then, at my request, she narrated the following:

"João, when he was not yet eight years old, became bewitched."

"Bewitched?"

"Yes; but listen. One day, late in the afternoon, he and I went to catch fish in the forest stream. And when I was busy beating with reeds the grass-fringes, where the fish love to hide, João disappeared. I cried, João, oh! João! and—nothing. After looking on all sides, I saw him not far away, bending over a tree trunk that had fallen into the stream. He laughed and talked of what I know not, nor with whom. I called him three times, but he did not answer. Then I made the sign of the cross, calling out, in the name of *Deos Padre*, etc. João raised his head, and told me that he did not hear me call him, that he was far, very far away, conversing with a being more beautiful than the sun.

"When João reached the age of fifteen, there never ceased to haunt our house a bewitching maiden. There," and she pointed with her finger to the side of the stream, "to that great palm yonder, that serves as a bridge every moonlight night, she came. Her eyes were like the evening star, and her hair was of gold, and waving like the lake when it is in foam. Her face was white, and her lips and cheeks were of the rose. At times she sang, and her voice was more tender than the voice of the *sabiá* [robin].

"What she said was in a language that I do not understand"; but, sighing, "João understands."

And continuing: "When the moon was sinking behind the forest trees, there came a cloud, white as silver.

"She soared aloft with the cloud to sport with the stars.

"Now, that João is entering upon his eighteenth year, she no longer comes; but at every nightfall he disappears by the path yonder, and returns with the dawn. And it is with the *lorelei* that he goes!"

"With the *lorelei*?"

"Yes; my son is lost; he will descend to the depths; he is *enchanted*."

"Come, Aunt Dorothea," said I, trying to console her, "we will *dis*enchant the boy. I have a remedy for this that the bishop gave me."

"Is it true?" said she, contentedly, rising to her feet. We set out by the same path in which João had disappeared at every nightfall.

The cock crowed for the third time. The waning moon balanced itself in space.

In the forest were strange phantoms—immovable shades. After we had gone on for half an hour, I spied under the dense trees a *tapéra*, or abandoned hut. It caused me a mixture of sensations to see therein two figures. Just then the moon in full glory emerged from a cloud. Oh!

I went away slowly, and slowly called Aunt Dorothea. "Aunt Dorothea, how is it that you told me the *lorelei* was white like the moon, and had hair of gold, and her lips and cheeks were of the rose?"

"It is true; what then?"

"What then! She is brown like the *sapucaia*, her hair is of jet, and her eyes are black like the depths of night." By the hand I took the old woman, and showed her a seductive picture. The next day we went to the parish church to look for the old priest. And I was the *padrinho* (the best man at a wedding).

A TALE OF THE GREAT RIVER.

CHAPTER I.

THAT day Mr. Espirito Santo da Silva returned home to dinner later than usual and in a very bad humor. Seating himself at the head of the table, in the cool attire of cotton shirt and trousers, his feet encased in *tamancos* (wooden shoes), he called out in a gruff voice for dinner.

A little negress, who had just emptied the last calabash of yellow *farinha*, by the last plate placed on the coarse white table-cloth, went to the kitchen, and, telling her mistress that the *pae-sinho* (little father) was at the table and wished to eat, returned with a bowl of broth and a plate of boiled meat. These she placed in front of Espirito, close to whom, seated on a bench the length of the table, was his daughter, a pale, pretty brunette, with black lustrous eyes and hair. Finally came his wife, Dona Feliciana, or, as her friends called her, Dona Felica,—a short brown woman with snow-white hair, who was dressed in a faded cotton skirt and *camisola*.

It was mid-day, sultry and oppressive, and the dinner passed on in silence. Mr. Espirito attacked successively the meat with its *tambaqui* sauce, seasoned with fragrant red peppers ; roast game of *paca* with vegetables of *mandioca* sprouts. This was helped down by an enormous quantity of *farinha*, which he threw down his throat with the tips of his fingers, and with no little skill and precision, acquired not alone from custom since earliest childhood, but inherited from generations of ancestors.

The girl, for the purpose, used a spoon, and with her father's unerring skill and precision.

As they were beginning the dessert, great yellow fruits of the *pacova* tree, also accompanied by much *farinha*, Espirito said to his wife: "Get everything ready, we are going away."

"Where?" she inquired, without further comment. "To the Parus. I have already told Antonio to provision the canoe. We must start as soon as possible, for fish is *matto* [wood] this year, they say."

"When, then?"

"To-day is Thursday. Then on Monday."

During this chill, brief conversation, Rosa, for such was the name of Mr. Espirito's daughter, appeared slightly perturbed. With her mouth full of banana, her half-opened lips still sprinkled over with *farinha*, a faint blush rose to her cheeks as she met her father's eye.

This passed unobserved, however, and all left the table. Rosa went to the parlor, seated herself by her lace "cushion," whose bobbins in her little hands jingled back and forth with a tinkling sound. Her father stretched himself out in the hammock, hung across a corner of the veranda, and, with his long *cachimbo* (Indian pipe) fallen on the floor, slept, and snored lustily. He was speedily accompanied by

Dona Felica, who had swung her hammock in the little alcove, between veranda and parlor. This last room—pompously called the saloon—was furnished with a dozen chairs of stiff, solid Portuguese manufacture, two great cedar trunks, painted dark green, with red flowering branches on their respective covers, and a great wooden oratory, painted blue with yellow lines to represent gold. From the wall hung two religious pictures, St. Sebastian and Sant' Anna, and a hammock swung in one corner. These made up the furniture of the room, tiled, like the rest of the house, with square red brick. Those two unmusical sounds reached the ears of Rosa, who, with an air not unlike the timid deer of her father's forest, as on the outskirts he pauses to know whether without fear or danger he may slake his thirst in the neighboring stream, pauses to listen. Certain that her parents slept, she hastened to the window and looked nervously out.

The long, narrow street of Obidos was deserted. It was the noon-day hour of slumber. Nature, as well as man, seemed lost in repose. The sun, from a blue, cloudless sky, poured down his fiery rays, casting electric scintillations in the air, that stifled the very senses. Doors and windows of the two rows of low, uneven houses were shut fast. Now and then the faintest of breezes stirred the fronds of the *mucajá* palms.

A great red ox grazed tranquilly on the village green, his ruminating cud the only sound that broke the intense silence, save the rustling of blue and green lizards combating with one another for innumerable tiny insects. Even shops and groceries were half closed, the clerks, while their patrons slept within, nodding lazily over the counters. Soon after Rosa had gone to the window, a young mulatto girl came down the street. Her blue and yellow-skirt was tucked up on one side, between dress band and the warm palpitating flesh, while her *camisola*, almost sleeveless, hung far below one shoulder, revealing, with unconscious immodesty, neck and bust. She was on her way to the *igarapé* for water, the red jar for which she carried uprightly on her head. In a corner of her mouth was a short pipe. As she passed she turned round, grinning maliciously as if she knew Rosa awaited some one. And, indeed, shortly the figure of a young man appeared at the corner of the street, whom, with a swift motion of the hand, the girl beckoned to her, while he hastened his footsteps. Reaching the window, a low, rapid conversation ensued; she now and then stealing away to watch within, he glancing about in all directions, both with the vague unrest of evil-doers.

Rosa told him of their departure, of her despair at leaving him, him for whom she cared so dearly, and implored him, for the love of God and the dear Virgin, to fulfil the promise to which he had sworn. With his eyes fixed on the ground he listened to her agonized appeal in silence. Over his lips played a fine, ironical smile. Finally he answered: "I cannot marry now. If I did, the *patron* would show me the door, and I cannot afford to brave his anger— Have patience—I care for you well—Patience—

But now, *adeos*—You know the bad tongues" (*má linguas*). He pressed her hand tenderly, yet still over his lips played the same faint, ironical smile. Rosa followed his footsteps with sad, dejected looks, and as he turned the corner without once looking round, she dropped, with a peevish gesture, the straw curtain which swept the window-sill with a jarring sound. It was time. The hour of *siesta* was passing, already doors and windows were opening, and people were appearing in the street.

Until Rosa was twelve years old, she had lived on her father's farm at some distance from Obidos. This was a fair property, consisting of some 5,000 cocoa trees, besides excellent grazing grounds, which Espirito inherited from his father, who, in his turn, had inherited it from the grandfather, one of the first colonists of the place. The house in nothing could be distinguished from other houses round. It had the same long front, in whose thick clay walls opened four rectangular doors, and was divided into four compartments of equal size, communicating one with the other by chinks, covered in lieu of doors with *japás*.

At one side was a straw-covered hut, where was the oven with all the appurtenances for making *farinha*. On the other, was the great *tendal* for drying cacao.

In front of the house were tropical shrubs, fruit trees, orange, *sapotilla, copuassú*, passion-plant, and there was one stately cocoa-palm, whose fruits were especially dedicated to Saint Antonio. A calabash tree threatened with its great round fruits the security of an old canoe, raised up by four sticks from the ground and filled with earth, in which were planted, as if in a hanging garden, all sorts of flowers in a discordance of color and perfume.

On all sides stretched out the sombre shadows of the great *cocoal*. This farm, as is a rule in the Amazon, bore the name of a saint, which, by the way, indicates no sign of any particular religious sentiment on the part of its owners. It was called Saint Isidoro, for what reason is not known. For a long time Espirito seldom left its precincts unless to go to town on election day, or for some festivity or other. Here Rosa was born, and grew, and romped and played under the cocoa and orange trees. Her father, an ignorant man, who could little more than read or write, still had much common-sense marred by great indolence, the vice of all Amazonian settlers. He married early, without passion or even interest, a neighbor's daughter, to whose house he had become accustomed as a bachelor. Dona Felica, a superb, voluptuous specimen of *mameluca* girl, with all the defects and good qualities of that race, possessed not only greater physical strength than her husband, but far more ambition and activity. When she was young (*moca*), meaning until her sixteenth year, she was tender and caressing in all her words towards her husband, but with a tenderness and affection purely sensual. This, after a time, merged into respect, even fear, and, finally, into the passive submission of a slave. Still, she possessed over him the superiority of the worker. She it was who directed the labor of the house and the farm, planting the *mandioca*, making *farinha*, helping to gather cocoa, and on the fishing excursions taking even a hand at the oar. Two years passed after their marriage before the birth of Rosa; certainly her parents were·fond of her, but would have deemed it no poignant affliction had she never been born. At nearly the same time an Indian woman in the house gave birth to a boy, and to her was given the care and nursing of Rosa, who grew up, if not a robust, at least a healthy child. She lived a half amphibious life between beach and water. She built tiny huts in the sand in which to shelter and swing in bits of hammocks her dolls, made either by mother or nurse —monstrosities still interesting as works of primitive art. To her moral education little attention was given. She was rarely punished, except in cases of disobedience or insubordination. In the *sala* before mentioned was an oratory, covered with coarse, deformed images. Partly through teaching, partly through observation, she learned that they were called saints, who lived with the Father in Heaven (*papae doceo*), also that when she cried they were displeased. She noticed that they were seldom approached except in case of thunder, or family affliction, when a candle was lighted and placed before them, or even a jewel, or a bright bunch of flowers. So she sometimes on similar occasions placed her playthings on the oratory. Once she saw her Indian nurse, who had lost and could not find a golden ear-ring, beat, in a sudden access of fury, a certain Saint Antonio, beat him vigorously with a twig of the *cipó*, and then turn his face in disgrace towards the wall. As they told her, when she cried, that the saints and our Lady did not like crying or naughty children, she began to fear them, and to eye them timorously from afar. For about the same reason, she was frightened at the *currupira* and the *tutu*, wicked black witches who devoured naughty children. The nurse, or Indian mother (*mac-tapuia*), as Rosa called her, was accustomed to sing her to sleep with Indian rhymes, not wholly unmusical. Later, she told her stories of ghosts and goblins, of wood-elfs and forest nymphs, so that no wonder the poor child confounded savage superstitions with the history of saints and the teachings of Mother Church. These last were initiated by Rosa's grandmother, who taught her to make the sign of the cross and to repeat the *Ave Maria* and Lord's Prayer. At night, tired out with play, she generally lay down in the same clothes she had worn during the day. Finally, in an evil hour, at the urgent request of some political friends, the father decided to move to Obidos, where he would hold some slight position in the Common Council. Rosa was rejoiced at the change, but experienced a certain depression of spirits at the loss of her old companions and wild liberty of action. This, as she was placed at school, wore away, where, being quick, she made rapid progress, and at the end of two years, she had learned all that was in these parts deemed necessary for a woman to know. She had her catechism by heart, she knew the elementary branches, and could sew, embroider, and make the country lace to perfection.

On her way to school, Rosa had to pass the shop of a certain Manuel Bicudo, to whose clerk, Antonio, had been given the same surname. This clerk was an evil-minded fellow, feared by the peaceful Obidenses, on account of his malevolent tongue and the calumnies he so cunningly invented and set into circulation. Unhappily, Rosa did not know his real character, and had she been told it is doubtful whether any impression would have been made on the volatile mind of the girl. Moreover, Antonio was very good-looking, with the supple frame and great languid eyes of the Peninsula. Whenever Rosa passed, followed by the *mae-tapuia*, who carried along her little tin box of books and sewing, he never omitted to pay her some simple compliment, which, she, proud of her conquest, smilingly received. Now she, like others of her precocious schoolmates, had some one to love and to love her. As to the *mac-tapuia*, whose heart Antonio had won over by presents of cotton cloth, pieces of tobacco, and cups of *aguadente* so agreeable to the Indian palate, she even favored these attentions, and one day took from her belt a letter filled with protestations of love which Rosa speedily answered. And at this time Antonio really seemed to have lost his head over Rosa. At mass his eyes seldom left her, and it seemed an ecstasy for both, that silent interchange of glances. He still loved to assume airs of the sceptic, and at the church fair, dedicated to Sant' Anna, he offered, to the horror of the devout, a *sagui* (small monkey) which he had bought for ten *milreis*, to this favorite saint.

With the facility which small places offer for making acquaintances, he began to frequent the windows of Espirito's house, now conversing with him, now with D. Felica, then with Rosa, who at first was shy and silent.

He accepted, one day, a proffered cup of coffee, and entered the dwelling. His fine airs and graces finished the conquest of D. Felica, at whose "orders" he had already placed the shop of his *patron*. Of this acquaintance Espirito did not disapprove, as it permitted him to open a credit therein. By these means Antonio gained over him the superiority of a creditor, which afforded him a still freer access to the house, and he began to woo the daughter openly. The mother to this paid little attention, and she knew just as little of her daughter's nature, in which already could be detected possibilities of that terrible *abandon* with which a woman, regardless of risk or duty, can give herself up, body and soul, to the man she loves. Things were at this pass when Antonio was suddenly dismissed from his place. In his pocket were the "economies" of years, made, be it understood, at the cost of his employer's money drawer. In a letter to Rosa he accused her of being the cause of his disgrace. The *patron*, he wrote, had forbidden him to visit her father's house, and neither would he trust him for a single *vintem* (cent) more. Of course, loving her as he did, he, Antonio, refused to comply with this arbitrary request, and had been turned out. This story, which the nurse confirmed, Rosa believed. The idea that she had made a victim not only caused her vanity to overflow, but redoubled her love. She had caused a human being to suffer—here—this poor fellow was persecuted on her account. She loved him more passionately than ever; her increased affection taking the form of maternal tenderness, which is at the bottom of every woman's heart. Poor fellow—in a foreign land—far from kindred and friends—and now unhappy—all for her. Ought she not then to protect him with her love, to console him with her caresses? He had sacrificed himself for her. . . . Alas! from Antonio had not been hidden this vehement access of passion. He became, in consequence, exacting, feigning jealousy, which flattered the poor girl, seeing as she did in this a new proof of love. Then he spoke of an interview—he was again employed, and very busy —he wished to speak to her alone—of their marriage—and much that lay near his heart. She refused, at which refusal he became angry, declaring that she did not do as he wished, because she no longer cared for him—he knew she cared for some one else—one João de Gomes.—She did not love him, Antonio, and he had been silly in sacrificing himself for her.—He would go away to the Madeira River, and it would be her fault if he died of the fever.

Then, for days, he never passed the door. They were sad only for Rosa, torn to pieces by the conflicting desire of seeing Antonio, and talking with him at will, and the dread of her parents' wrath were she discovered. And she thought of a plan by which nobody should know of their meeting. She had been accustomed to bathe in the little forest lake, with the *mae-tapuia*, and here he should appear as if by chance, and they could talk together. The *mae-tapuia*, to be sure, would not leave them alone, and she might suspect they wished to speak of things not meant for a third person's ear, but then she was silent and discreet. And this plan carried out— they sometimes met. Time passed, when one day Rosa received a note, saying that to-morrow would pass the steamer *Tapajós*, and that if she continued so obdurate, well—then he would take his passage by her—so then an eternal farewell from him who had loved her well—the ungrateful one! This blotted letter, with its disguised handwriting, bore no signature. Antonio's resolution, terrified Rosa. The idea of losing him maddened her. She would send him a message at once. Going to the kitchen, she took from the coal basket a piece of coal, which she wrapped round with a thread of the *tucum*, into which she had fastened eleven knots. Hiding this, wrapped up in paper, in her bosom, she seated herself at the window, waiting an auspicious moment for sending this singular message. Presently, a little *tapuya* passed, a sickly, demented-looking girl. In her arm was a bottle, in which, probably, to purchase rum, at the *venda*.

"Are you passing Sr. Antonio's store?" asked Rosa.

"Sim, Senhora."

"Here take these four *vinteys* [four cents] for *doces*, they are for you, and take this parcel to Sr. Antonio, and say ' by the old garden-gate.'"

"Sim, Senhora."

Antonio received parcel and message. At first, he could not understand the former, but finally it dawned upon him that the coal meant night, and the eleven knots in the *tucum* the corresponding hour. And he laughed a laugh, worthy of the Evil One himself.

. . . .

All in Espirito's house slept—all except Rosa. Feverish with fear and waiting, she had counted the hours until now the old kitchen clock sounded out eleven. In the same white dress she had worn during the day, pale, barefooted, her black hair waving over her shoulders, she slipped out into the garden. The night was clear and humid. The moon, like a golden globe in the clear blue sky,. bathed all nature in light. Silence reigned, broken by the discordant howl of a dog which, from afar reached Rosa's ears. At the rough garden gate, of *acapú* sticks, she paused tremulous, nearly senseless.

She felt an arm encircle her waist, and on her cheeks, already humid with the dews of night, were pressed hot kisses. She instinctively shrunk and withdrew. Still, every nerve of her body, quivering in that opulence of cold light, called out for warm, suffocating caresses. She felt prostrated, as if before some mystic vision. Then he whispered in her ear, low, tender, supplicating words. She scarcely had strength to shrink farther away.

"Are you deceiving me?" she murmured in a failling voice, and looking at him with a great tenderness.

"I am not deceiving you; I swear by this moonlight that is bathing us in its heavenly radiance," he replied, touched in spite of himself into momentary earnestness.

"In the name of God," she continued, "you promise to marry me."

"In the name of God"—imprinting on her lips a long kiss. The dog from afar gave one last discordant howl; a bird from a neighboring tree sent forth one wild, sharp note; the moon under a passing cloud hid her face of glory; and nature was hushed into oppressive silence.

. . . .

That night Dona Felica was disturbed by a noise in her fowl yard. Hastily rising, without removing her night clothes, she examined the place. All was quiet. Withal, it seemed to her that near the garden gate moved two figures—one of a man, the other of a woman. She was proceeding thither, when again the moon hid her face under a cloud, and all was wrapped in gloom. At the same time, the howl of a dog resounded from afar, and the wailing note of a bird in the tree overhead sounded out like a groan. Dona Felica, always superstitious, crossed herself, ran hastily to her room, sprinkling over her face a little of the holy water yet remaining in the calabash. Then the moon came out in renewed glory, and it seemed as if all in the house of Espirito slept.

CHAPTER II.

On the identical Monday which has been mentioned, Espirito set out with his family for the Parus, where it was said this year the *pirarucu* abounded. What obliged him to leave the charm of town life and the honorable occupation of his calling was dire necessity.

With little foresight, he had left his farm, abandoning with it his only legitimate interests. He had run into debt and was obliged, in order to rescue the property from seizure, to make the annual fishery. On this account he had returned home in such a bad humor on the day he announced his determination to Dona Felica. He had become accustomed to the idle life, to the disputes and debates and babbling talk of the little town. Home he seldom came except to meals or at bedtime. Outside of the Council sessions, he was generally to be found at shop doors, or at the apothecary's shop, the great meeting-place for gossip and political intrigues.

As for the farm, it was going to rack and ruin. Espirito had let it to an old Indian, an idle scamp of a fellow. The crop produced little, and half that little was robbed.

On the morning of their departure, Obidos presented a gay appearance. The semi-monthly steamer had arrived, a great event in the early days of the opening of the Amazon. Through curiosity, or to receive or send unimportant cargoes, people came for miles around to see it. The town's entire population, men, women, and children, turned out, and when the great anchor was cast, the steamer was surrounded by canoes. Many came simply to compliment the captain, or commander, as he was called in those times of the Amazon Co., an important personage enough, with a superb disdain for these simple country people. Still, were he in a good humor, he would narrate the news of Pará and the south, generally affecting an intimacy with the " big ones" (*figuroés*). No end of presents were brought him—cakes, *doces*, monkeys, parrots, fruits, rare woods. After the distribution of the mail, groups formed at the corners of the streets, or in front of the town hall, where letters and papers were shown and news discussed. Many of the passengers went on shore; one of them, a highly tatooed Indian chief from the Purus, showed all the native indifference to the sights of the town. He was returning from a visit to the President of Pará, whom at a formal session at the palace he had astonished beyond description. According to some preconceived Indian idea of etiquette, on his Excellency's head he had placed his flaming head-dress of feathers, while on his own rested the sober black hat of that dignitary. A tall, thin English naturalist, with yellow beard, and wearing enormous blue glasses, gesticulated in impossible Portuguese around his luggage, on the top of which perched a garrulous parrot. By frantic signs and gesticulations an Indian porter was made to understand that the *senhor* and his luggage were to be taken ashore.

Under the awning of the great canoe, Rosa, with palpitating heart, watched the scene. She looked towards the town, half hidden from view by great Brazil-nut trees, at the beach, at the water, where men and women alike waded knee-deep to fill their rude jars with water. For him, for whom her eyes were searching, she looked in vain. No one came.

The canoe was let loose at a good, safe " broadside" from the steamer, and soon Obidos, its white beach, flat houses, and outlying forest, faded into the distance. Rosa's last hope was dispelled. Miserable and humiliated, down her cheeks ran the swift-flowing tears. Her parents attributed hêr grief to the pain of leaving town, and left her to herself.—It would soon pass over. The girl's sensations are difficult to describe. She experienced neither remorse nor sorrow, but a scorching fire of fury, that she had given herself up to one who evidently cared no longer for her, whom, alas! she loved more dearly than ever.

The voyage to the fisheries passed uneventfully enough. Once only the canoe stopped, and this was at the mouth of a picturesque *igarapé*, in order to cut *estejas* (long sticks of even length) for the hut, as by the lakes were to be found none of these materials.

The *Parûs* to which Espirito went with his family is, in the fishing time, not one lake alone, but a conglomeration of lakes, some fifty in number, known collectively by that name. Like all the Amazon coast region, it presents yearly two widely distinct aspects. In the rainy season, or during the general overflow of the Amazon, whose despotic influence is felt by all waters connected with it directly or indirectly, the *Parús* is one vast lake, whose length has not been accurately calculated. In summer or the dry season, islands submerged for nearly five months rise from the waters fresh and verdant, leaving in their wake lakes of varying forms, depths, and sizes, all connected together by *igarapés* or channels. And where months before had passed some steamer, are (erected on the higher banks of these *igarapés*) traders' huts, and on the lesser lakes fishermen ply their tiny canoes.

Still, in summer as in winter, water is the predominating element; the air is saturated with it, and at night one is wrapped around by the overcharged dew, as with a wet mantle. On these margins, less swept by the furrows of canoes, rises a superb aquatic vegetation. At certain distances this girdle of green is spotted by beaches of black earth, frequented by legions of gorgeous butterflies; at a distance, and in repose, appearing like flowers springing from the black soil. Millions of tiny birds revel in this vegetation, among the leaves and flowers from which the *bóto*[1] loves to wreathe garlands for his victims.

Isolated in the tranquil lakes nearer *terra firma*, the Victoria regia (Jacunda's oven of the natives)

---

[1] *Bóto*, a fish which, according to the Amazonian legends, takes the form of a beautiful youth. His voice is low and full of melody. Alas for the Indian maiden who in the witching moonlight hears it and flees not!

unfolds, bordered round with a vivid carnation, its enormous semi-spherical leaves. Rising a few inches above the water, fragrant past all sweetness, are its flowers: in the morning, white as a heron's wing; at evening, a tender rose-pink, which finally deepens into red. Despite its seclusion, the Victoria regia, through its wild, savage beauty, its extraordinary size, will ever dominate over all the aquatic world's flora.

Lazily floating on these same lakes may be seen hundreds of alligators, as lazily waiting for worthless pieces of fish thrown into the water by the fishermen. When these pieces are not thrown with sufficient force to reach the water, the alligators quickly come ashore for them. Famished *urubus*, which with men and dogs also emigrate hither at this time, perched on trees, or walking along with slow, rhythmic step, bide their time for the share of the feast. It is droll to watch these birds, as now they half fly, half hop along, cawing meanwhile with their disgusting *chem-chem*, then soaring aloft above the stone throws of some naked little *caboclo*.

If here vegetable life, confined to a few species (which, however, flourish with rare luxuriance), lacks the forest opulence of lands not subjected to river inundation, animal life, however dependent upon the individuality of *terra firma*, teems with magnificent prodigality. In the midst of *canarana*[1] are thousands of birds, which fly rapidly away at the approach of footsteps. There are the *piassócas* of earthen color; the slender grass-birds, of

[1] Wild grass as high as the sugar-cane.

seven colors; overhead soar aloft flocks of snow-white egrets; joining together at times in flocks of hundreds to make their *tinguijadas*, or fishing parties, to some far-distant stream.

There are ugly yellow *arapapas*, with their enormous concave beaks, larger than their heads; deadly serpents coiled together in immense masses; green clouds of parrots; *japins* with their long nests hanging from the silk-cotton trees, not unlike rows of brown Christmas stockings. There is the ugly *carachui*, in ugliness and song unrivalled; the *saracuru*, whose strange notes startle the unaccustomed ear, and the native canary, not unlike a golden humming-bird.

At dawn of day the fishermen set out in their canoes, and the lakes present a lively appearance. In the prows can be seen men attired only in trousers dyed in *moruchy*, consequently the copper color of their own skin. By the side, ready to plunge into the flesh of the great *pirarucú* as it unwarily floats by, rests his harpoon. At this time not only does this fish abound in the lakes, but an infinite variety of others, for which the Indian, with his quick eye, awaits with half-stretched bow and arrow. Especially animated was the fishing season this year. Espirito quickly put together his hut, in whose construction, be it noted, not a single nail figured, strong *cipos* serving the purpose.

CHAPTER III.

TRY as she might, Rosa could not forget Antonio. He was always present to her imagination, yet she was now convinced that he intended to deceive her. And fear took a thousand dark-hued shapes.

One morning, as she sat on the trunk of a *mongubeira* tree, the *japins* twittering overhead, a canoe passed by which was presently moored near her father's hut. In the prow was a young fellow dressed in foreign-looking clothes, and wearing a straw hat of a foreign manufacture. It caused Rosa an inexplicable shock, the first sight of that figure. Yes, there was Antonio. He jumped ashore, and stood only a few steps from her, bowing and smiling. The color rose to her pale cheeks, while her heart beat fiercely within. She had not the strength to fly. He pressed her hand tenderly as he whispered: "I have come on your account—ungrateful one!" At that moment the father, who had not gone that day to the lakes, called out: "Ola, is that you, Antonio? Then you have come to the fisheries? Rather late, though. What's the news in the town? They say that Pacheco has been condemned.—How is my *compadre*, the captain?—Nothing new from Pará? —Then we have won the election, eh?"

The young man replied to these and other questions as best he could, finally accepting an invitation to breakfast at Espirito's house. Antonio equivocated when he told Rosa that it was for her sake he had come. In truth, he had no longer any affection for the girl. Satiety had brought weariness—the death of love. When the family had left Obidos, his strongest sensation had been one of relief. He did n't wish to marry any one yet, certainly not Rosa.

He had been surprised by an order from his *patron* to prepare for the lakes. Besides the purchase of fish, he wished him to collect some outstanding debts. For this he was given a canoe, money, and provisions. At first he had wished to excuse himself, but according to the terms of his contract could not well do so. And, then, what had he to fear from Rosa, or her poor devil of a father, against whom he had a strong weapon, the recovery of a debt of 300$000. And so he had greeted Rosa smilingly with a lie on his lips. Despite her paleness she had changed into a more voluptuous beauty, and he smiled to himself at the thought of renewing their old relations. They would last, he said to himself, well—as long as the fishing season, perhaps longer. But Rosa had strangely changed of late in her feelings towards him, and his declarations now fell on wearily indifferent ears. This unexpected resistance, while it exasperated Antonio, rekindled his old passion, and he resolved to again engage in his favor the *mae-tapuia*. He complained bitterly to her that she was an ungrateful girl; that at much personal inconvenience he had arranged this voyage to gain something, the sooner to establish himself, and to marry her.

The *tapuia*, whom a cup of native rum had considerably softened, assured him that he was mistaken, that her foster-child cared for no other, and that he could count on her.

"Does she never speak of me, Aunt Thomasia?" asked Antonio.

"Never," she replied, "but what of that? And she is ill; one night I had a bad dream about her"—and with a sudden suspicion—"I was even capable of thinking you had done her some harm, Sr. Antonio."

"I, Aunt Thomasia? *Por Deos*, no!—But listen. You speak to her of me. See that she comes here to-day, under this *sumaümeira* tree. I want to arrange our marriage, you know. I have much to talk over with her. After mid-day, then, when Dona Felica is sleeping.—Yes,—here, take this price of *chita* [calico]."

The *mae-tapuia* returned home with the price of calico, and after putting it away in a *balai* (coarse basket), which served as a trunk, went to look for Rosa, who was idly swinging in her hammock. Sitting on the *tupi* mat beside her, she related what Antonio had said.

"Heaven deliver me from him!" exclaimed Rosa irritably.

"Why, child? He is a *bom sujeito* [good fellow], and cares much for you."

"He does not. He is very wicked!"

Was it from despair, was it from the old childish

instinct that the *mae-tapuia* could help her,—be it as it be,—Rosa, bursting into a flood of tears, told her all.

. . . .

The *mae-tapuia* did everything in her power to soothe the agitated girl, and at once instinctively formed her plans. Remorse found little place in her bosom, and in reality, outside of her petty venality, she had wished only to do the young people a service. Rosa she had nursed at her breast and loved as her own child. And if, as she affirmed, Antonio really cared nothing more for her, and would never marry her.—*Ai*—the only thing that remained was—well—one of those thousand *pussangos*—potions in vogue in the country. No one knew more of these potions than did she, thank Heaven! But one difficulty remained. In the meadows about grew none of these herbs, only in the *terra firma*. This would not baffle her. No! There was her son, Rosa's foster-brother, he should go to the *trombetas* for them. All settled, she comforted Rosa as best she could, enjoining on her to not lose hope—she would arrange all.

Only two days after was Thomasia able to speak with Antonio, and then she besought him, with more feeling than one who knew her would suppose her capable of showing, to repair the wrong he had done Rosa by marrying. To his villainous words in reply she listened as if turned to stone, but finally rising, half strangled with fury, furious as a wounded tiger of the outer forest, she hurled at him the curse of her race.

●

That same day the *mae-tapuia* entered Rosa's room, carrying in her hand a black, glossy gourd, from which the girl uncomplainingly drank. She did not lament, nor complain, neither for her fault in itself did she feel any compunction. Of late she had been dully thinking of Obidos, of her schoolmates, of the old gossips,—they would point their fingers at her, if they knew. And these things spread about quickly in small places. She now feared everything; if a visitor appeared, she was found seated silently at her work at lace-cushion. She shuddered when she remembered her father; perhaps he would beat her, and the idea caused her to turn faint and giddy. Later she fell into an apathy, scarcely fearing even her father's wrath.

Some two weeks after Thomasia's interview with Antonio, the latter knocked at the door of the hut. It was Sunday, and all were within. "*Entre com Deos*" (Enter with God), called out Espirito in answer to the knock. Antonio came in, giving all as usual the time of day. He quickly saw that nothing unusual had occurred within. He had come, he told Espirito, on a business advantageous to them both. He knew that he had some thirty *arrobas* of fish to sell, and he would like to buy it. Others paid in goods, he would pay in cash. He would give something over four milreis, for each *arroba*. The money was ready in his canoe.

"Too little," replied Espirito, "I have been offered five milreis an *arroba*."

"Who offered it?"

"João Periquito."

"That I doubt. In goods perhaps, but not in money."

"Well, decide at once, *pregai oŭ largai* [let or leave it]. Sr. Antonio, you must give me five milreis."

"*Safa*, but you are mean."

"Fish in Pará is dear, ten milreis an *arroba*, they say."

"Lies, my friend, all lies, it is not so dear."

"And you know, with freight duties, and what not, scarcely a percentage can be made," replied the clerk, in that droning, complaining voice he had learned from the traders. Silence succeeded.

During this dialogue Rosa had not once glanced towards the young man. It was mid-day, the hour of dinner. The little negress, Camilla, with whom we are acquainted, entered the room, and over the straw mat, extended between the hammocks of Espirito and his wife, spread a small, coarse cotton cloth.

This was a Sunday luxury; on working days the family ate from the mat, on the floor itself. The cloth, with its blue earthenware, horn-handled knives and forks, and its leaden spoons, was laid. Two calabashes for each plate served, the one for water, the other for parched *farinha*.

Antonio, watching these preparations, was about to leave, saying: "Well, will you let me have the fish? If so, I will send the man for it. *Adeos*."

"Don't go yet. Afterwards we will talk of business. Stay and eat."

Antonio consented, with the condition that

Espirito would not refuse a flask of wine which he had in his canoe, and for which he asked leave to send the little negress. Duly arriving, they seated themselves at dinner, which was composed wholly of fish. Antonio sat at Rosa's side, and moved by a sudden impulse to hear her speak, offered her some wine, which she brusquely refused and shortly after left the room. Espirito, however, did not refuse the wine, and at the close of dinner his eyes had grown alarmingly small, and his speech heavy and slow. Now this was a propitious moment for Antonio to speak of the purchase of fish. He would n't let it pass, and talked as before, perhaps with more warmth. Espirito, half tipsy, finally consented to the other's bargains. Under the influence of the wine he had become tender, even obsequious. He would not hear of Antonio's going away. It was Sunday. Nothing was doing. There was a hammock stretched out by his own. He must have a siesta, and overcome by heat and a good dinner, both speedily fell into a heavy sleep, as did the good D. Felica.

And without, nature slept, the silent sleep of a midday under the equator.

CHAPTER IV.

Quite an animated crowd that afternoon had assembled in front of Espirito's hut, near which he stood with his family and Antonio. Some were standing, others were seated on rough wooden benches, or the outspreading roots of the great *sumaümeira* by the bank. The stream was nearly deserted. Perhaps it was owing to this fact that, for the last quarter of an hour, an enormous *pirarucú* had been sporting in the waters, sending them up in clouds of crested foam.

"Ah! my fine fellow," said a half-Indian, squatting on the ground not far from Antonio, "you see that nobody is about, and that is why you are so sportive. Just wait a bit, till I set out with my harpoon."

"In truth," said another fisherman, "he seems disposed to have a tussle with somebody."

"He is large, the *bicho*" (animal), observed a third.

"Yes, he would weigh at least three *arrobas*" (*arroba*, 32 lbs.), said another, practised in the art of calculating weight at sight.

"How he beats about, just to taunt the alligators," remarked another, of which some half-dozen were in sight.

"I have a great mind," said Antonio, "to harpoon that fish."

"You, Sr. Antonio," challenged the *tapuio* who had spoken first. "That *bicho* is not for you, *meo branco*" (my white man).

"Why not?" asked Antonio, somewhat nettled in his self-love. "It would n't be the first I 've caught. Three days ago, ask João Domingos, I harpooned one in Bouiçro."

"That may be, *meo branco*, in the day of the *uaiva*, when fish are *tonto* [giddy], but not in this time of the moon."

"Go to the devil," was the angry response.

"I will wager two *pirarucús* against a demijohn of *cachaça* [rum], that you can't get that *pirarucú*," insisted the *tapuio*, and he laughed again that peculiar, indigenous laugh, showing in full the red gums and the white pointed teeth. He was joined in this by his companions, which irritated Antonio still more, and he was about to retaliate, when turning round he caught Rosa's glance of quiet scorn. White with rage, "Pedro," he called out to a native, "lend me your canoe. I will see whether or not I can bring that *bicho* to shore." The *tapuio* consenting, he proceeded forthwith to unfasten the canoe.

"Don't be foolish, Antonio; you will lose that flask of *cachaca*," observed Espirito, seriously.

"That 's none of your business," replied Antonio, jumping into the canoe. This was in length little more than twelve feet. Squatting in the prow he rowed quickly away.

The *pirarucú* was now only a few yards from his right, and with two vigorous strokes he had gained on it sufficiently to be out of the reach of its first leap. With one foot firmly placed before the other, eyes fixed, harpoon in right hand (in all trying to imitate the native), he stood ready. On shore the group watched silently. Occasionally a rapid observation, favorable or otherwise, was hazarded, as to the young man's manœuvres. Some, among others was Rosa, had risen to their feet. Suddenly, from each breast burst forth a loud cry. Two or three men sprang into one of the lightest boats and set out rapidly. That had been an anxious moment, in which Antonio awaited the *pirarucú*. Concentrating all his strength, he had thrown the harpoon, but in the narrow prow lost his balance and fell overboard. In his first plunge he had failed to grasp the canoe, which had indeed been driven outward by the force of the fall. He was a poor swimmer, and besides, the weight of clothes, which never hampered the native, pulled him under. Half strangled with the water in his throat, he called for help. A monstrous alligator, its black back and extended jaws plainly visible, glided in his wake. . . . A blood-curdling cry rent the air. Canoes, rowed by Indian arms, shot forward with the velocity of arrows. Too late! The enormous amphiboid—eighteen feet in length—had already seized Antonio by the arm, and was swinging him round with the velocity of a wind-mill. Blood dyed the water in great circles round. And at sight of this the terrible *piranhas*, with their razor-edged teeth, famished, blood-thirsty little creatures, by thousands—yes, millions—swarmed over, under, about that mutilated body in frightful warfare with the alligators and one another.

Canoes that came to the rescue slowly returned. When told the particulars, Espirito with the instinctive hatred of the conquered for the conqueror, as instinctively exclaimed: " Why did this devil of a Portuguese, then, meddle in what he did n't understand?" And this was Antonio's funeral oration. At the moment the alligator had snatched off Antonio's arm, Rosa, who had stood as if petrified with one cry, fell down in a dead faint. Her mother and Thomasia carried her to the hut and laid her in her hammock. The faint lasted long in spite of much vinegar, burnt cloths, and other remedies in vogue. Then a fever set in, and a prostration that lasted the night long.

CHAPTER V.

ROSA lay white, immovable, like one dead. D. Felica's face wore a startled, idiotic expression, as if in the presence of some great mystery. She was sitting on the straw mat by her daughter's hammock, and every now and then repeated in agitated tones: "*Commadre, commadre*, what then is this?" Aunt Thomasia, whom she addressed, did not at once reply. She was busily arranging this, putting that in order. Finally she replied: "Quiet, Sra, *Commadre*, quiet. I don't know what I think. I believe it is the work of the *boto*.[1] Don't you remember what happened that night in the *quintal* at Obidos? What you told me? That form which rose to the clouds when the *matin-tapereira* cried? And after that night Nha Rosa went about as disconsolate as a tortoise without a mate. Don't you remember? And her appetite, too, fell away. She was always near the river, under the *sumaúmeira*. I went there, and, to be sure, saw nothing, but I think the *boto* called her thither. That fish has the cunning of the Evil One. It was he who brought evil on Lopes' wife, when her husband went to Pará. And poor Loló, whom he carried away, as she slept by the river, and who has never been heard of to this

[1] The fish before referred to, which at times takes the form of a seductive young man.

day. And in that spot one can hear the mournful song. He is always on that river—the other day I saw two *botos*, sporting one with the other, the evil creatures. For me it is the *boto, commadre,"* concluded Thomasia, who, during this discourse, had also seated herself on the mat, and spoke low in order not to awaken Rosa, or that she might not hear.

D. Felica listened without interrupting the *tapuia* —listened incredulously, resignedly. She believed the *boto* quite capable of doing this evil deed. Many times she had listened to similar tales. She remembered that night in the *quintal*. Then that bird was watching and had given the signal, and the *boto* had ascended. In her daughter's life which she passed in review, nothing occurred to arouse suspicions. Yet, as her faith was not a living one, rather a lingering belief, she could not root out a certain fear or distrust. Rosa awoke, turned in her hammock, looking confusedly about as if in search of something, and again fell into a deep lethargy. D. Felica resolved to have her daughter blessed. Thomasia knew of an old sorceress, or dispeller of evil spirits, who enjoyed great fame in this respect, and went in search of her. The sorceress was of the same opinion as the *mae-tapuia*. She blessed the girl, making the sign of the cross over different parts of her body, and murmuring low, incoherent phrases, finally expelling the *boto* in the name of the Father, etc. The next day Rosa was better, and D. Felica, placing a candle in her hand, made her repeat a prayer on her rosary before the image of N. S. das Dores (Lady of Pain), which image she always carried with her in her trunk, the cover of which served as an altar for the devotion. From this time Rosa commenced to grow thin and pale, in fact, became almost ugly. She went about with the air of one in disgrace. Her father noticed the change and questioned the mother as to the cause. "It was the *boto*," replied D. Felica without entering upon a description of the habits of this extraordinary creature. Espirito, just then very busy with the municipal elections in which he finally gained a more important position, paid little attention to the subject. In Obidos, where soon after the catastrophe the family returned, not all were ready to credit the miraculous version which, notwithstanding the watchfulness of the *mae-tapuia*, somehow had crept out. Especially, Sundays at Mass, the young men who watched Rosa curiously as she entered the church interchanged malicious glances and smiles.

AMAZONIAN LEGENDS.

COMPILED BY PROF. HART.

HOW THE TORTOISE OUTRAN THE DEER.

A JABUTI met a deer and asked: "O deer, what are you seeking?"

The deer answered: "I am out for a walk, to see if I cannot find something to eat. And, pray, where are you going, tortoise?"

"I am also out walking; I am looking for water to drink."

"And when do you expect to reach the water?" demanded the deer.

"Why do you ask that question?" returned the tortoise; "I can run faster than you can. If you are long-legged you cannot run as fast as I."

"Then let us run a race," said the deer.

"Well," answered the tortoise, "when shall we run?"

"To-morrow."

"At what time?"

"Very early in the morning."

"*Eng-éng*" (yes), assented the tortoise, who then went into the forest and called together his relations, the other tortoises, saying: "Come, let us kill the deer."

"But how are you going to kill him?" inquired they.

"I said to the deer," answered the tortoise, "let us run a race. I want to see who can run the fastest." Now, I am going to cheat that deer. Do you scatter yourselves along the edge of the *campo* in the forest, keeping not very far from one another, and see that you keep perfectly still, each in his place! To-morrow, when we begin the race, the deer will run in the *campo*, but I will remain quietly in my place. When he calls out to me, if you are ahead of him, answer, but take care not to respond if he has passed you." So, early the next morning, the deer went out to meet the tortoise.

"Come," said the former, "let us run."

"Wait a bit," said the tortoise, "I am going to run in the woods."

"And how are you, a little, short-legged fellow, going to run in the forest?" asked the deer, surprised.

The *jabuti* (tortoise) insisted that he could not run in the *campo*, but that he was accustomed to run in the forest. So the deer assented, and the tortoise entered the wood, saying: "When I take my position I will make a noise with a little stick, so that you may know I am ready."

When the tortoise, having reached his place, gave the signal, the deer started off leisurely, laughing to himself, and not thinking it worth his while to run.

The tortoise remained quietly behind. After the deer had walked a little distance, he turned round and called out: "*U'i yanti*" (Hullo, tortoise!). "Well," said the deer to himself, "that *jabuti* does run fast!" Whereupon he walked briskly for a little distance, then cried out again, but the voice of a tortoise still responded far in advance.

"How's this?" exclaimed the deer, and he ran a little way, until, thinking that he surely must have passed the tortoise, he turned about, and called again, but "*U'i suasa!*" came from the edge of the forest just ahead.

Then the deer began to be alarmed, and ran swiftly, until he was sure that he had passed the tortoise, when he stopped, and called; but a *jabuti* still answered in advance. On this, the deer set off at full speed, and after a little without stopping, called to the tortoise, who still, from ahead, cried, "*U'i suasa!*" He then redoubled his forces, but with no better success, and at last, tired, bewildered, he ran against a tree, and fell dead. The noise made by the feet of the deer having ceased, the first tortoise listened. Not a sound was heard. Then he called to the deer, but received no response. So he went out of the forest, and found the deer lying dead. Then he gathered together all his friends, and rejoiced over the victory.

THE CURUPIRA.

(*Curupira*, a being who lives in the forest, and leads people astray, that he may destroy them.)

A MAN was hunting in the forest; led astray by one of these beings, he lost his way, and at night went to sleep at the foot of a tree. The *curupira* came up to him, and beat on the *sapopema* of the tree; the man awoke.

"What are you doing here, brother?" asked the *curupira*.

"I was lost, and I remained here," answered the man.

"Then," said the *curupira*, "give me a piece of your heart to eat!"

Fortunately the man had killed a monkey; with his knife he opened its body, and cutting out a piece of the heart, he gave it to the *curupira* who ate it, supposing it to be the man's heart. "It is very sweet," said the *curupira*; "give me the whole!" And the man gave him the rest of the monkey's heart. Then he said: "Now, you must give me a piece of your heart." The *curupira* thought that if the man could cut out his heart, he also could do the same. So he asked the hunter to give him his knife, cut open his own body, and fell dead. The man, free from his enemy, fled. After a year the hunter remembered that the *curupiras* have green teeth, so he went to get the teeth of the one he had killed, to make a string of beads. He found the skeleton at the foot of the tree; taking the skull in his hand, he struck one of the teeth with his hatchet, when, to his amazement and fear, the *curupira* stood alive and smiling before him.

Thank you, brother, for having awakened me!" said the apparition. "I had lain down a moment to sleep." Then he gave the man an enchanted arrow, saying that with this he could kill any game; but he charged him not to tell any one from whom he had received it. Heretofore this man had been a bad hunter; but now he killed much game every day.

His wife, noticing this, asked him how he had become so expert.

The husband at length told his wife all, and immediately fell dead.

STORY OF THE JAGUAR WHO WANTED TO MARRY THE DEER'S DAUGHTER, BUT WAS CUT OUT BY THE COTIA.

A JAGUAR had a mind to marry; he fell in love with the daughter of the deer, and one day he asked and obtained the deer's consent to the match. Now the jaguar had a friend, the cotia. So to the cotia's house he ran, in great joy, to tell the news and boast of his good luck. "See how fortunate I am!" he cried. "I am going to marry the deer's daughter, the prettiest girl of the forest, and you, my friend, shall attend the wedding!"

"You are indeed happy," responded the cotia. "I congratulate you!" But in his heart he was resolved to cut the jaguar out. So when the jaguar was gone, he ran to the deer's house, and asked for his daughter in marriage.

"I would be very happy to give her to you," said the deer, "but she is already engaged to the jaguar, who asked her of me but now."

"Poh, poh!" exclaimed the cotia, "the jaguar isn't good enough for her; he is only a miserable old dotard, the worst beast in the woods, and the weakest; why, I could make him carry me, for all he is so big!"

"Say you so?" exclaimed the deer. "Well, cotia, if you can make the jaguar carry you, you shall have my daughter." So the cotia went away and awaited his opportunity. When he knew that the jaguar was going to the deer's house, he went and lay down in the path where the jaguar must pass; and had a bandage round his head, and he pretended to be very ill. Presently the jaguar came by, and saw him.

"Hullo, cotia," said he, "what are you doing there?"

"I am lying in the woods," said the cotia, "because I am very ill."

"I am going to see my betrothed," said the jaguar; "get up and come along with me."

"Indeed, I would like to," sighed the cotia, "but, as you see, I am quite unable to walk."

"Well," said the jaguar, "if you will come with me I will carry you."

"Very good," responded the cotia, "if you will carry me I will go." So the jaguar took the cotia on his back and walked off with him.

Presently the cotia slipped off on the ground. "Oh, cotia," said the jaguar, "why did you fall off?"

"I fell off," answered the cotia, "because I am so weak that I can't hold on."

"Well," said the jaguar, "I will tie you on with *cipó*." So the jaguar got a *cipó* and tied the cotia fast to his back, and so went on. Presently the cotia began to strike the jaguar with his fore-feet."

"Hullo!" exclaimed the jaguar, "what are you striking me for?"

"I am striking you," said the cotia, "because you have n't given me a switch; every one who rides should have a whip."

The jaguar, willing to humor his friend, gave him a switch; he used this very gently until they neared the house of the deer, when he began to whip with all his might. The jaguar, mightily enraged, tried to shake him off, but the *cipó* held him fast, and together they ran through the forest. The cotia waited until he saw a hole; then he gnawed the *cipó*, and slipped off, and so got into the hole before the jaguar could seize him.

The jaguar watched at the mouth of the hole for a long time, but at length he became very tired and thirsty, so he said to an owl: "O owl, will you watch this hole for me while I go and get some water?"

"Yes," said the owl, "I will watch it for you and nothing shall escape."

The jaguar went off to drink, and the owl sat watching the hole. Presently the cotia peeped out and saw the two great eyes staring at him; he threw a handful of sand into the owl's face and blinded him, and while the latter was rubbing his eyes, the cotia got out of the hole and ran away.

Just then the jaguar came back. "O owl!" said he, "where is the cotia?"

"Alas!" answered the owl, "he threw sand into my eyes and blinded me, and then ran away!"

After that the jaguar could never catch the cotia, and the mischief-maker married the deer's daughter, because he had made the jaguar carry him, as he promised.

THE BIRD OF THE EVIL EYE.

FAR away in the thickest forest lives the *tucano-yúa*, Bird of the Evil Eye. It has a nest in the hollow tree; from a crevice under the branches it surveys the ground beneath; if any animal passes near, the bird has but to look at it, and the evil eye does its work. All around the ground is white with bones. The bird feeds on its victims, and not even the strongest can escape it.

Long ago a hunter, straying farther than was his wont, found this tree with the bones lying white about it. As he looked, he saw the *tucano-yúa* peering out, but the bird did not see him, and ere it could turn its head, the hunter shot it, and it fell to the ground. The man approached the body carefully, walking so that he did not pass before the eyes; then with his knife he cut off the bird's head, wrapped it in a cloth, and put it into his hunting pouch. Ever after that, when this man saw a deer or paca or tapir, he held the *tucano-yúa's* head so that the bill was pointed towards the game, which instantly fell dead. But he took care never to turn the bill towards himself.

The man's wife wondered much at her husband's success in hunting; she questioned him often to discover the reason for this good luck, but he answered always: "This is no business of yours; a woman cannot know of these things." Still she was not satisfied; day after day she watched her husband stealthily. And once, when the man and his wife went with a party to the woods, she watched more closely; when a deer or cotia passed by, she saw that her husband took something from his hunting-pouch and held it toward the game, which instantly fell dead. The woman's curiosity tempted her to find what this strange weapon could be. It chanced after dinner that the man went to sleep on the ground. The woman approached him softly, opened his hunting-pouch, and took out the head of the *tucano-yúa*. Turning it about, she tried to recall her husband's actions.

"He held it so," she said to herself, "with the bill turned toward the game." But as she spoke, she had carelessly turned the head against her husband's body, and in an instant she saw that he was dead. Overcome with fear she started back; but in so doing she turned the deadly beak toward herself, and she also fell dead.

BE CAREFUL TO WHOM YOU DO GOOD DEEDS.

ONE day the fox was taking a walk, when he heard a growl—ugh! ugh! ugh! "What is that?" he said to himself; "I will go and see."

The jaguar saw him, and said: "I came into this hole a long time ago; I grew large, and now I can't get out. Will you help me to roll away this stone?"

The fox helped him; the jaguar got out, and the fox asked: "What will you pay me now?" The jaguar was very hungry. "I am going to eat you!" And he caught the fox, and asked: "How is a good deed paid for?" The fox answered: "Good is repaid with good. Near by there is a man who knows all things; let us go and ask him." They crossed to an island; the fox told the man how he had got the jaguar out of the hole, and how the jaguar in payment wanted to eat him.

The jaguar said: "I wanted to eat him because good is repaid with evil." "It is well!" said the man; "let us go and see the hole." So they went, all three. Arrived there, the man said to the jaguar: "Go in; I want to see how you lay."

The jaguar went in: the man and the fox rolled back the stone, and the jaguar was a prisoner again. "Now," said the man, "you will learn that good deeds should be repaid with good!" So the jaguar was left, and the others went away.

CATHEDRAL OF PARÁ, BRAZIL.

AMAZONIAN BELIEFS, TRADITIONS, AND SUPERSTITIONS.

THE Brazilian savage, be he of the great family *tupi-guarani*, be he of the *Tapuio* race, was, in matters of religion, at the time of the discovery of Brazil, in the fetish period. He scarcely even possessed superstitions. Myths, following the careless explanation of natural phenomena, gave rise to no other belief than the one of fear, and this a transitory sensation, ceasing when the cause thereof had ceased.

Similar characteristics may be observed in the *Tapuio*, the *Mameluco*, and other Amazonian races of the present day. Their religion is a mixture of *fetichism* and *polytheism:* this, received from the Portuguese; that, brought down from the savage. Catholics they are, merely in name, and because such they have been baptized. It is difficult to find among them one individual who is a perfect monotheist. The savage mind cannot grasp the elevated conception of Christian monotheism. If it has been able to digest anything in the Catholic faith, it is because the Jesuit missionaries, of all catechists the shrewdest and most able, have, in a manner, adapted the religion to the savage taste. They have introduced into their worship certain indigenous practices, which have rendered it more agreeable to the senses, consequently more accessible to the understanding; as, for instance, the creation of the *saire*, later on to be noticed.

These clever priests, not perhaps so well-intentioned as many other less successful missionaries, have comprehended the truth first established by sociology, that no single man, unprepared by natural evolution, can pass from fetichism to polytheism without taking along with him something of the remnants of the former; that on this account one should undoubtedly make before the savage the same *momices* (grimaces) as did the heathen *pages*,[1] as well as to conform, to a certain degree, to their understanding, the rules and discipline of the Church. This, then, may be the cause of their success, which, however, is somewhat more apparent than real, as will presently be shown.

Of the pretended *tupis* gods, none except the *jurupari*, the *curupira*, and the *matin-tapêrê*, survive in the imagination of these people, and these are mixed up with Catholic beliefs. They are considered an ill-favored, malignant genii. The first takes the form of the Catholic devil; the second is variously defined, but is still a demon; the third is a species of hobgoblin, who has only one leg, and is subjected to the influence of a horrible old woman, who, at night, accompanies him from door to door, begging tobacco.

[1] In order that the sermons preached to the Indians should produce more effect, and not appear less inspired or persuasive than the demoniacal doctrines preached by the sorcerers (*pages*), they endeavor to imitate their uses, making occlusions and visions, giving now and then loud cries, stamping the foot," etc., etc.—*History of Brazil*, by the Viscount of Porto Seguro.

Outside influence or superstition, principally Portuguese, has placed on the head of this being a bonnet, or cap, confounding him with the troublesome *pesadelos* of the current Indo-German mythology in which he is so represented. In the nightly strife, who manages to snatch off this cap, will attain happiness.

The old woman, who leads him, sings to the rhythm of a bird, and this song, incomprehensible in itself, is probably the remnant of some myth. It is as follows:

> Matinta Pereira,
> Papa-terra já morreu;
> Quem te governa, sou eu.

> (*Father* Earth has died,
> Who governs you, is I.)

The *Tupan, Uaraci, Jaci, Cáapora*, have died out.

The famous *page* or sorcerer, the medicine-man (both, for the savage, are the same), and the soothsayer of the *Tupi-guaranis*, survive the gods of whom they desired to make priests. The actual *pages* are generally born and reared far in the interior, surrounded by forests rich in medical substances, whose virtues, partly through teaching, partly through experience, they learned to know. Aided by the profound faith of their sick people, the results prove generally favorable; perhaps *faith* assists the cure. These cures are generally accompanied by Catholic rites; this further to strengthen belief in the power of these *pages*.

And the looker-on in the exercise of these *medical-religious* functions can witness dancing—such dancing round the patient—to the sound of a cymbal, while mysterious words, that are to save, are murmured.

In more civilized centres, like Manãos and Pará, the sorcerers dispense with these ceremonials, but surround themselves with much mystery. In Manãos, not many years ago, a *page* was called upon to treat a patient, but refused to do so, except at night, and with closed doors. Besides, the *page* is the *benzidera* or blesser, to whom reference shortly will be made.

Knowing little or nothing of the solar system, these people still have a sort of astrological belief, based probably on the direct and all-powerful influence of the moon on terrestrial objects. During the eclipse of the moon, August 23, 1877, the people of the capital of Pará made an enormous uproar with old tins, fireworks, cries, fire-engines, and even gun-shots, to put to flight, as they expressed it, that devil (*bicho*) who wished to eat the moon.

The *bóto* (*Delphinus pallidus*), the Indian *uyára*, occupies a large space in the imagination, and the Amazonian region is filled with marvellous histories of this animal. The *bóto*, like the mermaid of old, sings, and its song is full of enchanting melody.

Woe to the maiden who lingers in its spell! The Indians believe that at times this fish assumes the form of a youth, who carries away the maiden in his arms, and to this fluvial Don Juan is attributed certain consequences that such imprudence would entail. This last belief must have sprung from a woman's imagination,—a woman who wished to conceal a fault that, in some tribes, is still terribly punished. Withal one should not thoughtlessly accuse that generation in which sprung up certain beliefs of insincerity, nor yet the present one. Be it as it be, the belief in the *bóto* firmly exists. Not long ago, a person, in the sincerest good faith, told of a *bóto* who, assuming human form, carried away an Indian girl from her hammock, who from that time had never been seen.

Other versions of the *bóto* or *uyára* have obtained credence. He, at times, jests with people, bringing up objects from the depths of the water to show them. One was seen with a knife in his mouth, from whence brought is not defined. He causes canoes, in which are young girls, to be wrecked in order to possess himself of them. And, at times, he assumes a woman's form and casts over some gallant youth a fatal spell. The eyes of this animal are considered as precious amulets to soften lovers' hearts. The teeth are excellent preventives against infantile diseases.

A member of the same family, the *tucuxy*, is said to be a great friend of man, whom he often succours from the grasp of the *bóto*, thrusting him along by his snout, until he reaches the bank of the stream in safety.

The Amazonians believe in *cured* persons *(pessoas curadas)*, *i. e.*, that they may be rendered invulnerable to the bites of poisonous snakes and fish. The secret of this cure is known only to the *pages*, and by them has never been disclosed.

However, a popular superstition has it that if the head or tail—extremity of either—when half alive, be eaten, the bite from its species is rendered harmless. Quite recently, in Santarem, a *tapuio* killed a small snake, eating its head and tail nearly raw.

The Amazonian Indians believe that a snake can seldom miss a gun-shot, and also in the metamorphosis of the *surucucú* *(Trigonocephalus lanceolatus)* into the *paca* *(Cœlogenus fulvas)*. The *surucucú*, they say, is a heavy sleeper, and of this fact the *pages* take advantage in surrounding him with a sort of hedge, and covering him with ants of a certain species, thus transforming him into a sleek *paca*. The fact is, that the *surucucú* takes shelter in these ants' holes, on whom, perhaps, they subsist, and in which also come the *paca*, with whom it is known they enter into a sort of comradeship.[1]

The *sucurijú* *(Eunectes murinies)*, or the great snake, is also the object of a superstitious belief. It is said he appears at night on retired lakes or streams, frightening away with his eyes of fire (one the distance of a foot from the other) the boldest fisherman. The gun with which an *urubú* *(catharites)* is killed becomes useless.

The possession of the bird called *uirapurú* is considered an efficacious talisman against ill-luck. Until a few years ago it was rare to find in the interior a *venda* (drinking-place and grocery) that had not

---

[1] In 1749 Fonseca writes: " A fellow passing through the woods, wishing to secure an animal somewhat larger than the rabbit, called the *paca*, in order to do so was obliged to thrust nearly the length of his arm down the hole, where it was hidden. He secured it at the cost of having his first finger cracked asunder with the teeth of a venomous snake, called the *surucucú*, which species is so intimate with the *paca*, that from this alliance is derived the Tapuian fable that these *pacas* are offspring of the *surucucús*."

the skeleton interred under the floor nor hanging from the wall. It is difficult to take this bird alive, consequently its value is very great; a dead one costs over thirty milreis.

The skin of the nocturnal bird, *jurutani*, preserves maidens from harm.[1]

Formerly these birds were killed, the skins removed and dried in the sun, over which, during the first three days of womanhood, the girls were obliged to sit, and were meanwhile visited by the matrons of the tribe, who enjoined upon them virtue and sobriety. At the end of this time the damsels were supposed to be *curada*, *i. e.*, invulnerable to temptation. To-day, according to different accounts, it is more customary to sweep the floor under the bride's hammock with the feathers of the *jurutaiu*, which will accomplish the same end, *i. e.*, tranquillity of spirit, and will guarantee the virtue of the future wife.

[1] Herewith is a description, given by an old Brazilian author, of this bird. "Of all light-shunning birds this is the least timorous. He is long and slender, and of a brownish color . . . his cry is shrill, like a burst of mocking laughter. He stretches himself out on a tree as if part of it, and there he lies motionless, allowing himself to be taken by the hand at will.

" Is it not interesting to observe the correlation existing between the complete quiet of the bird and the peace the savage mother wishes to invoke for her daughter? She, too, must sit motionless over its skin. . . . The fact of correlation of beliefs with habits or modes of the object which gives rise to such beliefs is one of the most fascinating theories of mythology. In addition to what has been related of the *jurutani*, there are in Amazon-land many other birds which are invoked for tranquillizing purposes, among others, the *quatipurú*, of all the greatest sleeper, and whom nurses call to their aid when children refuse to fall asleep."

Among the Amazonians is current a vague belief that the monkey was once a man, which, without doubt, is a lost echo of a *tapuian* generical belief. It is said that certain individuals, as a punishment for treachery, were transformed into monkeys, of whom it is recorded to this day that they don't talk because they can't row.[1]

Of the Indian tribe, *Ugina*, it is said the men have tails of two or three feet in length . . . covered with a leather-colored skin without hair.

The beliefs which have for their objects *vegetables*, are generally those whose properties are medicinal. And for the people who entertain these beliefs, the great Amazonian forest is an enormous drug store, in which can be found remedies for all " ills flesh is heir to." Superstition, of course follows in the wake of these beliefs. The *tajapurá* (aroidea), placed in the prow of a fishing canoe, will, according to tradition, ensure its owner good-luck. Another aroidea, *juruti-pepina*, serves as a body (*corpo*), in which is sheltered a mythical bird, who sings near one without being seen, and is near one without being felt.

One can see the plant, with its beautiful green leaves, striped red and white, and can hear the bird-song, but can never discover the bird. To the Indians this plant is an object of great terror, so much so that they will not allow it to be spoken of with contempt. And he whom this fabulous plant chooses as the object of its malignity, will become paralyzed. In fact the word *pepina* signifies in *tupi-guarani (pe)*

---

[1] To not row, is in this fluvial region a seeming impossibility.

which breaks, *(piu)* that which paralyzes, that breaks or inutilizes arms, legs—in short, that paralyzes.

The beliefs referring to minerals, are nearly extinct, with the exception of the celebrated clear green stone, the *muèraquitan*.[1] Still one finds now and then, an old woman who will sell this stone, which, in the guise of an amulet, is hung from the throat, together with the rosary, and with teeth of animals. Of similar dangling objects, mothers, even those who are civilized, will suspend from the necks of their children, from cord or chain, serpents' teeth, birds' beaks, shells, eyes of Saint Luiza in metal, figures of Saint Braz in bone, all to preserve from mortal disease, from falls, the evil eye, convulsions, blindness, etc., etc.

If children fall ill, they are blessed by *pages* or old women, to whom is attributed the occult and mysterious science of a cure by means of blessing.

One of the formulas of this process is the following:

> " In the name of the Virgin,
> Bewitching evil eye,
> Go forth from here,
> This child is not for thee."

[1] This stone was fabricated by the *Amazons* (female warriors) . . . In olden times, at Santarem, an Indian rite was practised, principally on the mandioca settlements. In the centre of the mandioca field, a stone was placed, called the *mother* of the mandioca, which served as an altar for various sacrifices and ceremonials, and which was guarded with the greatest care.

Was an old Brazilian author justified, then, in declaring that stone-worship formerly existed on the Amazon?

It is said the *muèraquitan* loses its virtue, if set in gold or metal.

The *tupi-guaranis* believe that everything has a mother (*ci* in their language). The river, the woods, the mountains,—all have their *mother* or *ci*.

A traveller, hearing a strange noise, asked an old woman what it meant. "It's the *mother* of the *mamorana* (carica)," she replied. The *mamoranas* are plants, that grow in fields along the banks of the streams. The wind, passing through them, bends their heads like rushes, and their heavy leaves, beating one against the other, produce the noise heard, which, according to the opinion of the old woman, was the " manifestation " of the *mother* of the plants.

Some kinds of flies are mothers of certain plants, and when those insects die, the plants fade and wither away.

Such are some of the beliefs which the Amazonian people inherit from their savage ancestors.

As has been remarked, their religion is rather a mixture of fetichism and polytheism, than monotheism. The beliefs arising from the *tupi-guarani* faith are fetish; those from the Conqueror, polytheistic. Withal, fetichism always predominates.

It is not uncommon to see these people dedicate a bird, an animal, or the fruits of a tree to some favorite saint.

In Monte Alegre a traveller was unable to procure one single bunch of cocoas, as they had all been dedicated to the patron saint of the village.

Near the town of Obidos, at a small agricultural establishment, was one tree, whose fruits were exclusively dedicated to St. Antonio. Often on the *sitios* (farms) it is impossible to buy, for example, a fowl. One receives the simple answer, given without excuse or explanation "It is for the saints "—*E'do santo !*

Withal a saint, among them, is often the victim of reproach and insult. When rain is wished he is plunged into the water ; when anything is lost he is tied up, beaten, and exiled from the oratory.

The belief of one God, "Three in one," is almost unknown. Indeed the name of God is seldom heard except in phrases like the following: " God preserve you " (*Deos o queira*), or " If God wishes " (*Si Deos quizer*). And in their minds is the Holy Spirit no other than a saint, certainly the object of much festive devotion, owing, it may be, to his favorite and beautiful symbol, the dove.

Neither has Jesus Christ for them the importance assigned in Catholic theology. He, like the God-Child (*Menino-Deos*), is simply an object of fetichism. It is a shocking fact, but nevertheless a true one, that the Supreme Being, Triune of Christianity, holds little place in the minds of the Amazonian races. For them the saint is all—the object of all their religious sentiment, poor and fanatic as it may be. And even this saint is partly transformed into a *tapuian* god similar to the one their forefathers worshipped.

Among those beliefs which are ranked as tupis—Catholic, belongs the *saire*. This is both a profane and a religious ceremony, comprising the mass, the song, and the dance. The song is a melopoeia, sad and monotonous in the extreme. Herewith two verses: (1) *(Tupi)* " *Itácamutí pupi neiassucá pitaní puraga ité.*" Translation: "In a stone font was baptized the Child Jesus. (2) *(Tupi)* "*Cunha puraga imembira raue catú iputira ipópe.*" Translation: "Santa Maria is beautiful among women, and her son is like unto her." Each verse is droned by three old women, and all join in the simple refrain, "Jesus and Santa Maria." After the song is concluded refreshments are passed around.

The word *saire* signifies crown, and the ceremony is very old. The dance consists of short paces, like the soldier's quick march, performed to the sound of a tambour which is generally played by an old Indian.

This feast, or ceremony, if not created by the early Jesuits, met at least with their approval. One of the earliest Jesuit missionaries composed hymns for the Indians in their language, in which God, the angels, and the saints are praised, and better to attract through the melody of the hymn, he himself taught those of the young who possessed the best voices.

The acuteness and perspicuity of the Jesuit fathers thus stand revealed. They well understood the necessity of this mixture of rites against which the Indians would not rebel as against the teachings of pure Catholicism, for which their minds were totally unprepared. Yet, on one hand, if the Fathers succeeded in subjugating these wild people, and far better than the metropolitan government with all its power; on the other hand must be attributed to them, at least to a certain point, the amalgamation of savage fetichism with Catholic rites.

One of the most popular feats in this respect is that

of the Holy Spirit (*Espirito Santo*). A month or two before its advent the *Imperador* (Emperor), for such is the name given to the Director, the Judge, Majordomo, and devotees embark in several canoes, all gaily decorated with red and white banners. In the centre of each canoe is painted a symbolic dove, another is carved on the mast-head of the respective masts. The Emperor bears the *corða do Divino*, (crown of the Divine), and the devotees, bedecked with ribbons and carrying tambours, go forth to collect alms for the feast.

This region is a perfect labyrinth of channels, creeks, and lakes, on whose banks are retired hamlets, and scattered houses. To these *sitios* (a *sitio* is a name given to any habitation outside the settlements) the flotilla of canoes is directed.

The traveller passing along one of these channels (*igarapés*) is often startled by an odd-like *bum-bum* sound. He is told that it is the "crown of the Divine," which is near. And turning some point in the stream he sees several canoes filled with men, women, and children; flags are flying, and tambours beating. It forms a picturesque sight in the midst of the savage landscape!

In each *sitio* there is a feast. The "crown," after it has been kissed and held momentarily over the head of each person present, is placed upon a table, over which is spread the best cover. Around this crown are placed rows of lighted candles. At nightfall is given the litany, an enforced, uninteresting function. Mass is read by the best-informed man present, generally in horribly mutilated Latin.

Then begins the profane part of the feast; there is always a small, and badly attuned orchestra, and dancing follows, sometimes for successive days and nights. The principal feast of the year is always given at the *emperor's* house and with all the difference in the world, one is involuntarily reminded of an old-fashioned donation party at the parson's. Heifers, calves, sheep, fowls, pigs, baskets of *farinha*, tapioca cakes, fruits, are taken,—indeed a little of everything goes along. A little of everything, except money, which is a rare commodity on the Amazon, where traffic is almost wholly carried on by the primitive system of barter.

Occasionally the final feast takes place at the nearest village, in which is held a fair of the objects collected in order to pay the expenses,—Mass sung and a sermon preached by the parish priest.

At Obidos was held this feast, which is thus described by a traveller. "It was not a moonlight night, but the sky was illumined by millions of stars among which softly shone down the 'sweet southern cross.' River breeze and forest odor agreeably blended. The population of the town, in festive dress, stood ready to receive the *crown*, and to accompany it in procession to the church. In the middle of the river, many canoes, adorned with arches of foliage and showily illuminated, approached the shore. Weird was the effect on that calm, starlight night; the canoes, whose lights were fantastically reflected in the water, and which were filled with *devotees*, whose song the hour and the distance softened into melody!"

A FISHING PARTY.

TINGUIJADA.[1]

Half-past four in the morning!

SR. MANOEL JOÃO, colonel of the settlement "Una," could be heard in his room, alternately coughing, wheezing, and beating the head of his pipe on the hard floor. The tide was approaching low water. Sr. Manoel proceeded to the veranda, his head wrapped up, like a Mussulman's turban, in a red handkerchief. Four lean dogs, wagging their tails, fawned and jumped about his legs in frantic delight.

From a *sacco do isqueiro* (tinder-bag) he took a flint, a piece of steel, and some native tobacco. Striking fire, he lighted his pipe, from which rose the odorous fume of the *tic-terra*. It is to be remarked that

---

[1] *Tinguijada* is a preparation of *timbó-assú*, mud, and poisonous herbs, which is applied to an *igarapé* (forest-stream) for the purpose of inebriating the fish, which then come to the surface of the water floating on their sides, gills open, where they are caught in *panheiros* (coarse baskets) without any difficulty. Generally, the giver of one of these parties invites all his neighbors, who wait about in canoes until the *tinguijada* has produced the desired effect, when they proceed to load their canoes. Afterwards at the host's house the fish is equally divided among the guests.

This sort of fishing is strictly but vainly prohibited by the municipal authorities. Of course, it involves a great waste of "the smaller fry."

matches are all very well in civilized countries; for the inhabitants of a forest or rivermen, who live in the closest contact with nature, subject at every moment to her froward moods, they are useless.

Above all to the fishermen, who are constantly "*entre a agua do rio e a agua do céo*" (between water of river and water of sky).

The tinder-bag can be wet a week without refusing fire. Should the canoe be submerged, which frequently happens, the poor fishermen, being obliged to dive like ducks, the well-tempered steel, at the bottom of the water, beats in the tinder-bag and produces fire. This is why the provident and practical Sr. Manoel, going to a *tinguijada*, strung on his arm his old *sacco do isqueiro*.

At daybreak, then, this gentleman, with a large escort, started out for the *igarapé*, called Luiza Grande. The *Caiaidra*, or, as he is called, *preparer* of the *igarapé*, with other Indian servants, were overlooking the *tapage* (covering) or damming of the stream, which had taken place the midnight before at high tide. The first *tucunari assú* flew promptly above the *pary*.

"That's the *mother*[1] of the stream," said Sr. Manoel, disappointed. "The brute broke my *pindal* last week."

To prevent new disasters, canoes were pushed just outside the covering. A shoal of *Tucanarés pitangas* were caught,—beautiful creatures, shining like spangles of gold in the crystal water. As soon as they

[1] In Indian tongue *ci*; the Indians believe that everything, forest, mountain, river, stream, has a *ci*.

knew they were prisoners they retreated to a certain distance and began, all together, to fly away. Then the canoes approached still nearer; Sr. Manoel rubbing his hands with content, as these fish were laden in the holds. An Indian girl, meanwhile, ran to the woods to gather fagots, with which she quickly made a fire to heat the *beijus* (tapioca cakes) and prepare coffee . . . Then began the real work of the day, the *tinguijada*. Great quantities of the poisonous *cipó* were lashed to atoms, over the surface of the water, which seethed and foamed far down the *igarapé*.

The fish were soon floating, and the maddening excitement of the sport began . . . To seize them as soon as possible—that is the thing—or soon they will descend to the bottom to die! Men and women worked together

But on these excursions, it is necessary to beware of the *arraias* (ray-fish) which inflict a sting that can knock a person senseless, or can even cause death. These *igarapés* are filled with them.[1]

He had been *cured*, *i.e.*, made invulnerable and could now with impunity tread on any number of them without feeling their sting. But Sr. Manoel, in his enthusiasm over the lucky fishing, sent discretion to the winds and jumped right out into the middle of the stream.

Suddenly through the forest echoed a cry deep as the *Miserere* of the *Trovador* :

"*Ai! Jesú! ai! ai!* help! *Jesú! ai!*

---

[1] The Carárára had already warned Sr. Manoel to not jump out of his canoe into the water.

the ray-fish. . . ." He was carried along to the canoe, roaring like a wild animal.

"Where is the flask?" cried one. The Indian girl mentioned, with her skirts rolled up like trousers between her bamboo-colored legs, stooped down to examine the wound. "Where is it, patron?"

"Here—there—here—*ai Jesú!*"—groaned the poor man, pointing to his ankle and turning his head away to not see the blood.

The wound, somewhat larger than a sixpence, and as round, was speedily stanched, to be presently cicatrized.

But Sr. Manoël João was confined to his hammock for a good fifteen days afterwards, and never again, it is to be noted, ventured, when leading a *tinguijada*, into the waters of the *igarapé!*

AMAZONIAN RUBBER IN "FIRST HANDS."

(Dedicated to the dainty maiden, of that lost rubber shoe.)

IMPELLED more by the force of the tide, than any impulse given to the great oar, José reached the bridge of the settlement. He carried with him a great "mould" of dark brown rubber, which with his own hands he had gathered and made. And in the good old-fashioned style, by slowly smoking the milk of the rubber-tree over a smouldering fire, fed with the hard nuts of the *tucumá* palm. . . . Now in the great rubber emporium, Pará, the soul of the princely rubber merchant is grievously vexed at the tricks civilization has taught many of these rubber gatherers.

Balls of clay, sand, and what not, are introduced into the *pranchas*, or "moulds," to increase their weight. To augment the quantity of milk, sap from other trees is mixed. And worst of all, to avoid the tedious process of preparation, the *seringueiro* (rubber gatherer) makes a blazing fire, and when the milk is liquid, puts in a kind of flour, and if this causes it to coagulate too quickly, acid like lemon is added, to prevent its consolidation. Consequently, the purity of fine rubber is greatly damaged.

But back again to the settlement. The principal trader therein was a keen-witted Portuguese, whose dwelling and store were in one rude habitation. The *seringueiro* approached the heavy, old-fashioned scales, and putting the "mould" on, the rusty balance weighed out ten kilograms (20 lbs.). The trader kicked it out into an inner room, cheerfully remarking to his customer, six kilograms—four goes out for *quebras* (loss). The *seringueiro* never reclaims against such a decision, in reality a shameful extortion.

Not alone in *quebras* is he cheated, but in the purchase of the merest necessities of life, and above all in the price of rubber at the capital.

When the poor man wishes to enter into business secrets, the trader reads him an invoice from an account current of the patron at Manãos or Pará, always ending up with the ominous word—exchange.

The rustic is credulous by nature, and when he hears the word exchange he is struck dumb.

To him it is the synonym of an all-powerful being, who in another world orders the rise or fall of rubber!

The trader walked to the counter, wetted his pencil with the tip of his tongue, and taking therefrom a piece of coarse brown paper, said, "Good, what do you want this time, José?"

Then commenced the transaction. Cachaça, or rum, candles, sugar, tobacco, matches, etc. All noted down against so much rubber.

As the *seringueiro* never has a balance at the traders; always a debit in his books, this fact, as a usual matter of form, was mentioned.

And with a *boa noite*, and promising a speedy supply of other rubber "moulds," José started on his way.

But this time against the tide, and each stroke of the great oar resounded through the air like thunder!

And it being St. John's eve, over the bonfire built round his hut, as he reached home, he jumped the usual three times for good luck!

SINHAZINHA !

Eight o'clock in the morning! Sinhazinha had gone to the balcony for a breath of fresh air. She had swept and dusted the little shop below, which she tended together with her mother, the Senhora Margarida Carneiro, widow of a custom-house official at Pará.

The Sra. Margarida, as was her wont, took her morning meal of coffee and beÿú rolls in the shop door, better to enjoy the morning air, and a gossip with "Aunt" Anastasia, the herb-seller in front.

A good old soul was "Aunt" Anastasia, from whose watchful eyes, however, were hidden few of the secrets of the neighborhood. Sinhazinha heard her say to her mother: "There goes Amaral. See, he is going to the office. That's a proper young fellow! A jewel. He is so good to his mother. Poor woman, a widow like yourself, Sra. Margarida. A good husband he would make your daughter!"

And Sinhazinha saw passing down the street a tall young man, fair and well-looking, in whose mild physiognomy, however, mingled an air of sadness and unrest. He walked on, looking neither to the right nor to the left, without the least idea of being known to the herb-seller, or that his footsteps were followed by Sinhazinha, in whose ears were echoing the last words of "Aunt" Anastasia.

And who might take her to be his wedded wife would n't be so very unlucky. Indeed, not. Sinhazinha, with her eighteen years, though she looked younger, active and laborious, would be no unworthy helpmeet. Amaral passed every morning, on his way to the office, without even raising his eyes to her, and with the same air of preoccupation. And in Sinhazinha's ears were ever echoing the last words of " Aunt " Anastasia. And she had added that " he was so good to his mother." She, too, promised herself that she would be kind to her mother ; though she certainly was not very amiable, nor had she ever bestowed on her much of maternal tenderness or love. Still it was strange he never even saw her. One day, indeed, he lifted his eyes, and glanced at her. How her heart beat! and she went swiftly up to her favorite balcony. The next day she did not venture to the door, fearing lest he should think she was waiting for him, and so form a poor opinion of her.

And it seemed as if " Aunt " Anastasia sometimes smiled maliciously. Heavens! of what was she thinking!

Of what " Aunt " Anastasia was thinking is not known, but it is certain that Amaral never again took the trouble to even glance at Sinhazinha.

Days and weeks were passing. She thought she observed a change in the physiognomy of the young man, that he seemed contented, almost joyous, and once she saw his lips part with a happy smile. She was ignorant of the cause, but a little after she knew all, overhearing a conversation between " Aunt " Anastasia and her mother.

"Amaral is walking on air," the former said. "He is going to marry. The betrothed is the daughter of his patron—very fine people." All was explained. "Probably the dot," she continued, "is n't large, but she will have a grand *enxoval*" (outfit); "and she is so *chic* and fair—a blonde."

"That is it," said poor Sinhazinha, with a despondent shrug; "I am so hatefully dark. He likes blondes, and hair of gold. Well, she could never care for another.

She received offers of marriage—yes, and good ones. Not all who passed the shop were blind, but she refused all, and her mother found no fault. Egoist as she was, she knew how much to be valued were her daughter's services—— The business was extending——they were very well to do.

. . . .

Amaral married; he frequented the theatre, and all gatherings, with his wife, quite a grand lady, dressed in the latest Pará fashions. Sinhazinha sometimes wondered if she were happy; for she thought she divined in her a certain touch of vanity, of frivolity, and indifference.

. . . .

Great joy in Amaral's house, a boy was born.

After some time, Sinhazinha saw, accompanying the wife, a robust young countrywoman, fantastically dressed, holding in her arms a fair and rosy infant. "If that baby were mine," she said in homely phrase, "I would nurse him myself!" But Amaral's wife had no desire for this. And in a little while, with her capricious temper, her selfishness, and extravagance, her neglect of household duties, so many dissensions arose in that household that Amaral's mother, a saint if ever there were one on this earth, thought it better to leave her old home for a new.

"Is it possible!" said Sinhazinha, upon hearing this piece of news from "Aunt" Anastasia. "Poor lady, so good, so kind. I think it should not be very difficult to live with her!"

One day Amaral passed dressed in black. His mother had died. "*Deos meo!*" sighed the girl, "what will now become of the poor boy!" And not without reason was she disturbed. The child, left almost wholly to the care of servants, was fast becoming spoiled. The mother neglected him, limiting her affection to feeding him with cakes and unwholesome sweetmeats.

The child, always pale and weakly, became stunted in his growth.

Meanwhile the father, to satisfy the demands of his wife, spent all his savings, and was obliged to devote many hours of rest to excessive labor.

Still the means of living grew more straitened. His wife alternately chided and blamed him, urging him to leave that tiresome place for Pará, the capital. There he could get a situation worth having.

Sinhazinha, who heard much of what was going on, thought if only she could enter the house unperceived, to put all in order—if only she could do something. But what could she do?

She watched the child closely as he passed every

day to school, beating his satchel of books against his little legs. Notwithstanding his stunted growth, he liked to run about the streets, and shout, and play. With his curly hair flying in the wind, his dark blue eyes, and winning smile, he was an attractive-looking little fellow. But it made Sinhazinha tremble to watch his antics, here running into the middle of the street, then calling out some rude name to a passer-by.

One day she heard a coachman shout: " Here, here, little boy, get out of the way!"

A carriage was approaching and the horses were going at full speed. The child heard the cry, ran, became confused, stumbled, fell down.

Sinhazinha threw herself under the horses' very feet and pulled the child up. By a miracle both escaped unhurt. Wild with delight she took him into the house. What kisses, what caresses she lavished upon him! And she persuaded him to stay a long time, saying as he went: "Now good-by; don't say a word to your mother, so that she will not scold you. And next time, more care!"

The little one said nothing to his mother, nor yet to his father. When the child passed alone she gave him tender smiles and bestowed upon him more caresses, Oh! what fond caresses! "One must n't expect too much in this world," the poor girl said. "Even a little happiness so seldom comes!" And, alas! with her this little was to become less! Two days the little fellow had failed to pass. He had died, one night, of convulsions. "The doctor came too late," said "Aunt" Anastasia, "but when did the mother ever look after anything, let alone the child? She should have seen the danger in time."

Sinhazinha's eyes filled with tears when she next saw the father pass. He had grown gray, looked worn and old. Was it possible she, the wife, only sought to probe the bleeding wound? Yes, it was possible.

And finally things reached that pass, to use the words of "Aunt" Anastasia, that he was forced to close his doors upon his once well-beloved wife. She long ago had deceived and betrayed him. He was now indeed alone. And Sinhazinha too was alone. Her mother, at the close of a tranquil old age, had lain down to her long sleep. Yes, both were alone. . . . And he continued to pass without glancing at her, without even knowing that she existed. One day, as she stood at the door, their eyes met. Was it chance, was it premonition? He lifted his hat and gravely bowed. She inclined her head and went within, suffocated. Over her saddened existence it seemed to her had opened one ray of light. He had seen her, he knew her! Poor creature! this ray of light was only to illume its close! That same day a neighbor's child fell ill of a fever. Sinhazinha according to her wont, went to nurse him and took herself the dangerous fever. During the three days of her illness, she showed much resignation. At the last, she made this request of "Aunt" Anastasia, that after all was over she would send Amaral a card of invitation to her funeral. He had seen her— he knew her. Amaral wondered at the card, but attended. He met "Aunt" Anastasia, now grown old and becoming more garrulous than ever. Upon his inquiry, she explained that it was at Sinhazinha's request she sent the card, and she told him who it was who once saved his child's life, adding that for ten years Sinhazinha had never failed to await him, as he passed her door to his office. " I saw it all, *Senhor meo* "—Sainted soul,—" she cared for you well—too well."

He gave no reply. But now every morning as he passes the deserted shop, he says to himself : " There was felicity—there was true happiness. I had only to have knocked at the door—but now all is over ";— a similar history perhaps, is that of many human lives !

AN AMAZONIAN FUNERAL.

IN the palm-thatched hut by the side of the river, old Francisco lay dying. Yet no one would suppose that therein lay a Christian soul, passing into the portals of death. It was more like a house of feasting. Coffee, a decoction of mandioca, *assai*,[1] and sweetmeats were hourly passed round. Such is the custom of the *roça* (settlement, clearing). When the *curandeiros* (wise men) declare a cure improbable, that there is no longer hope (although with God nothing is impossible), and this often for days before the light of life is extinguished, the house is filled with guests. In civilized places, much is spent for physicians, medicines, the funeral, the service. Here, nothing of this, but there are *the neighbors*. As I said, it seemed like a house of feasting. The girls, sitting or reclining on mats of braided palm spread on the floor (mother Earth), told stories and laughed. Suddenly, wiping her eyes with the back of her hand, there appeared at the door of the room a withered old woman. Laughter ceased, as all gathered round as if to question her, while she between her sobs stammered out: "I said those herbs were no good; he should have taken the quinine my cousin sent," which, being in-

[1] *Assai*, a fruit of the palm, crushed to a pulp and eaten with sugar and *farinha*.

terpreted, meant that the poor old man had passed into the rest of the Hereafter!

Reader, have you ever seen a tropical storm—a storm that falls generally late in the day, during the change of the "wet" season to the "dry," or the reverse?

The sky darkens rapidly, a dry wind sweeps over the earth, tearing off branches of trees and thickening all the air with their falling leaves. After the wind, comes the dense heavy rain. Suddenly the tempest is past. The sun peers through the clouds. Silence falls on all nature a moment before so fiercely stirred. So it happened in the house of poor old Francisco, in the hour in which he rendered up his spirit to the Almighty. After the old woman just mentioned had closed the door upon the visitors, there broke forth a perfect tempest of cries, groans, and tears.

Soon quiet reigned. Sobs and tears ceased. Only here and there could be heard an exclamation like the following: "Eight days ago to-day it was that he took his arrow-spear, the one hanging on the wall yonder, and he said to me, he said, ' My old woman, I am going to look out for a *tucunarí.*'" And she choked up with sobs. "Yes," said a half-Indian girl, who was leaning against the wall, " up there is the head of the creature." Hunters and fishermen of the Amazon are in the habit of smoking the heads of all large fish or game caught, and stowing them away in the straw and rubbish of the roof.

. . . . . .

The funeral preparations now commenced. In

the middle of the room, on a great mat of the *miriti* palm, was placed the corpse.

At this moment Antonio, the nephew, appeared, bringing in a cross, carefully wrapped round in a linen towel. As he placed it on a rude bench, he remarked: "Afterwards this must go to 'Aunt' Thomazia; she is going to have a baptism in her house." In the interior the cross is likewise used on all festive occasions.—As the cemetery lay at some distance down the river, the funeral hearse was a canoe, with an awning of the strong fibre of the *bossu* palm.

Under this was placed the body of poor Francisco, dressed simply in cotton shirt and trousers, his best clothes, or, as the natives say, "clothes to see God in."

To the sound of bitter weeping the company embarked; the young girls dressed in white, with cayenne-jessamine, and lilies in their hair.

The canoe glided on to the sound of the tide. As before, the sound of weeping soon ceased, and by the time the *anna*, or mixture of rum, went round, there were not wanting piquant jests and jokes, which these rustics, although ignorant, know well how to season with a caustic and malicious flavor.

. . . .

At a picturesque point of the river, reached by a flight of shaky wooden steps, the canoe was fastened. The body of the old man was placed in a grass hammock, and borne on the shoulders of two near relatives through the narrow forest path. In Indian file followed the procession. Reaching a spot where the woods grew the thickest, a sharp note pierced the solitude. It came from the throat of that strange bird, the *quin-quin-o*. He only inhabits the great forests of the mainland. His song—if song it can be called—those measured notes of lamentation, is weird in the extreme.

Upon hearing it, Antonio stopped to fire his gun into the air, meanwhile exclaiming: "Here goes your grandfather, you bird of ill-omen!"

Finally this strange, half-fluvial funeral procession reached the cemetery, called, in the native tongue, *The Rest*. In it was a simple chapel, in front of which was erected a great cross of hard wood.

They laid the old man to his rest, each one dropping on his grave a handful of earth. And Antonio murmured this funeral oration: "My good uncle, sleep in peace; there is one the less to eat *farinha!*"

DOLCE FAR NIENTE.

"There is no joy but calm."—TENNYSON.

OVER the turbid waters of the Amazon, rising and falling to the blue fleecy waves of the Tocantins, our canoe glides gaily on! There, in one of those bewitching islands, kissed by the sweet, warm breath of eternal summer, caressed by sportive billows and fragrant breezes, we come to anchor!

In the midst of cocoa-palms and shady mango trees stands a rude dwelling.

The furniture consists of one great cedar table, and rude benches are placed along the *adobe* floors. What of it? In the open veranda we swing our hammocks; a couple of American rockers, patriotically keeping time beside. A few other luxuries of civilization meanwhile are unpacked.

Come in, reader, you who on your luxurious couch tumbled and tossed the weary night long as you thought over that last unfortunate speculation. It went badly enough, to be sure; you can weather the loss, but not much more of "brandy and vexation."

Even now they are telling on your once iron nerves. —Let well enough alone—come—rest in this "summer isle of Eden!"

And you, martyr of dyspepsia, hasten hither.—

Fish and hunt to your heart's content the whole day long. After all

> "Other joys are but toys,
> And to be lamented."

In this open-air life your appetite will reach voracity. "Dyspepsia and despair" will "take to themselves wings!"

Herewith an Amazonian recipe for dyspeptics. Catch your fish or game *yourself*, netting skilfully besides a supply of great shell-pink shrimps.

Prepare, seasoning with salt, lemon, and odorous native pepper.

Place over a brazier of red-hot coals, which blow now and then with the native mat-fan.

To be eaten at leisure, and leisurely washed down with the spring-cold water of the *igarapé*.

. . . .

To you of the aching heart and the o'er weary brain,—here—nature will lull you to rest, perchance to forgetfulness!

A BALL IN AMAZON LAND.

"Good-evening, Miss Anica."

"The same to you, Mr. Gregorio."

"Your blessing (literally benediction), Aunt Chica."

"God preserve you for good, Manduca."

Other cordial greetings having been exchanged, the girls seat themselves on great *tupi* mats, and the men on long wooden benches. In one corner of the room is the family oratory, covered over for this festive occasion with a cloth of scarlet red.

The musicians, like King Cole's fiddlers, are three, the instruments being the wire-strung guitar, the fiddle, and the *cavaquinho*, or small violin.

Coffee with egg, sweetmeats, and *mucúru*, or native punch, are presently served round. In a few moments, the country dance begins to form. The young men, after conferring briefly together, approach the *tupis ;* each selects the girl of his choice, assists her to rise, and marches with her to the middle of the room.

These young fellows, though coatless, wear shoes and sport gorgeous cravats.

The girls are dressed in gaily-colored cotton skirts, and chemise-like sacques, falling a little below the hips. The hair is adorned with flowers, and high-backed combs. Each girl has managed to secure a fan, with which she toys with all the languid grace of a Spanish señorita.

The *beau* of the ball seems to be a young fellow of twenty, or thereabouts, tall, straight as an arrow, loquacious, and extraordinarily at his ease. "Mr." Sylvestre, for such is his name, reads, writes, and reckons; and throughout the island, is dubbed as a learned young fellow.

As the music is about to strike up, the host appears, and looking around with an important air, calls: "All in places, then. Who leads?"

"He is at the head there, Sylvestre."

"That is right; nobody gives such an air to the fandango as does Sylvestre." Contented to see so many of his neighbors around him, the good man advances to a *cabocla*[1] of middle age, and leads her towards the "set," remarking: "Come, my old woman, we will dance bis-a-viz with Sylvestre. That 'll be fun!"

The hostess, standing near Aunt Quiteria, is also a *cabocla*, tall and sympathetic. She is dressed in red cotton skirt, and white *camisola* so "blued" that it is difficult to distinguish the original color. From her ears hang the largest pair of ear-rings mortal ever beheld, of good Portuguese gold.

They were placed there in her girlhood, and were never removed, except when through their own weight they fell down, parting open the ears.

Thus they were now imprisoned in their *seventh* aperture.

In Holy Week, or when she was in mourning for

[1] Civilized Indian.

some relative, a piece of black cloth was sewed over them.

The music striking up, Sylvestre, like a commanding officer, shouts out:

" Balance."

" *Tour*."

" *Dama passa, cavalheiro resta !* " etc., etc.

With this ends the formalities of the dance ; and now begins the real fun of the evening.

" Walk of the *roca*," (settlement) is called out. Each puts his dusky partner behind him, seizes her by the arm, and bears her aloft, over his shoulder.

" *Olha cobra !* " (Beware of the snake). Each turns round, continuing the figure, contrary-wise. Presently this is exchanged for "*furtä-pares*," couple-snatching, and other grotesque figures, often prolonging *one* quadrille until the morning.

At a late hour appears an important character, the harmonium-player, a new arrival in this part of the island. Approaching the host, with somewhat perturbed visage, he inquires : " How is it, Uncle Chico, that you did n't invite *me* to your fandango?"

" *Uai!* did n't you hear the guns ? " retorts, rather scornfully, Uncle Chico.

The *roceiro* (settler) never sends out invitations. A gun shot at five o'clock in the morning, one at mid-day, and another at six o'clock at night, are sufficient to fill his house with guests.

Thus Uncle Chico's scornful question: " *Uai,* did n't you hear the gun of the *roça ?* "

. . . .

As a sort of interlude, the harmonium-player now

begins the *lundum*, mournful in tune and discordant in the extreme.

Still on tired ears sometimes resounds the refrain of that melody:

> " Nosso ceo tem mais estrellas ;
> Nossas varzeas tem mais flores ;
> Nossos bosques tem mais vida,
> Nossa vida mais amores."

> Our sky has more stars ;
> Our meadows more flowers
> Our woods more life ;
> Our life more love.

ORCHIDS FROM A TROPICAL GARDEN.

NEAR THE FOREST.

DAYBREAK. Perfumes from rare orchids fill the air, red passion-flowers strew the ground. Great blue butterflies elude the grasp. A dewy freshness is over all. Now the sun glows into fuller life. We will descend the forest path, where the forest stream meets the tiny lake, and in whose clear depths the *miriti* palms are mirrored.

An Indian hut stands by the margin. Indian children, in tiny shirts, come and go, and stretch their bamboo-colored legs in the sun. Now the mother, in gay-colored skirt and *camisola*, approaches the lake for water. With what superb bearing, the red, filled jar poised on her head, does she walk away!

Still we are virtually alone. Indian apathy never slackens; never is roused into curiosity; asks no questions. We are free to come and go.

A glorious dip—a stretch in the sunshine—a reverie—and home to our palm-thatched hut again!

A MORNING CALL.

INTOXICATING sweetness from clouds of snowy jasmines fills house and garden. In the drawing-room, with its bare floor of black and white *acapú*, lofty ceilings, and simple bamboo furniture, are seated two visitors. They are sisters,—neighbors,—who greet the new-comer warmly. One of these girls might pose as a study for Murillo's "Madonna." The other, too, is superb in her way, with fine flashing eyes, and dark hair that hangs in braids nearly to her feet. In all-unconscious grace they sit, and "soft Southern speech" falls musically from their tongue. But what does the elder girl hold in her hands? A great, practical bunch of jingling keys! (She must be the housekeeper.) And my Madonna? She has a mother-of-pearl opera-glass in *her* hand, and nestling in her sleeve is a pet *rouxinole*, that flits hither and thither from a bowl of fragrant roses.

These girls wear dainty white muslins, and with filmy lace of their own handiwork. What need of bonnets or gloves!

All this was long ago.

My Pará belle of to-day visits me in the finest French toilette, and at the hottest hour of the day, it being the fashionable one. She has more *chic;* she is more accomplished, it may be, than her sister of old, but I miss—well, I miss—the golden *rouxinole!*

FESTA OF OUR LADY OF NAZARETH.
(The Patron Saint of Pará.)

"THEN the lady will *assist*, this night, at the *Festa* of Nazareth? Ah, but it is *bonita*, the *festa!*"

So smilingly affirms my *cabocla* maid, Marie, whose smiles deepen over her brown face, as she receives an affirmative answer.

Can I describe the first impressions of this strange annual *festa*? A little white-washed church, its one cross pointing up to skies where is the "sweet southern cross"; in front, a large square, not regularly laid out,—in fact, not laid out at all, but illuminated by hundreds of gaslights until far after midnight; gorgeous fireworks, at which the stately palms themselves seem to unbend a little, and to nod approvingly. Around the tree-bordered square are countless little tables of fruits and *doces*, the sellers thereof laughing, chattering Indian girls and negresses, whose brilliancy of attire Joseph's coat of old could not well eclipse. The evening Mass at chapel heard, the *leilao*, or fair for charitable purposes, attended, a long hour passed in watching the novel crowd that pass and repass the wide *paseo* round, and down the beautiful, silent Nazareth avenue, homeward again.

A SUMMER ISLE.

NOT unlike an emerald, in uncouth setting, rises my fairy islet, fresh and sparkling, from the turbid waters which gave it birth. Ay, not many centuries ago! On—over the tiny beach of sand, under trees of fragrant *cajú* and golden orange, by " palms in cluster,"—to where mango shades woo, and cooling breezes caress!

Pressed close to mother Earth, I dream, and am happy. Love breathes o'er the fragrant hours. Doubt, and pain, and sorrow, what are they? Less than yonder fleecy cloud floating over the mango trees, the turbid waters, and the fairy islet, Tatuoca!

AT REST.

" To where, beyond these voices, there is peace !"

IN a lone cemetery by the tangled tropical forest is a grave. There *he* rests! Over that grave willows never weep; birds sing never; flowers bloom not, for they wither in the fierce sunshine, or the raging tropic storms cast them away.

But the "sweet southern cross," the cross *he* and I have so often watched, looks peacefully down on that grave. What, then, if willow weeps not; if white flowers bloom never; if tropic birds in the forest have no song? My thoughts are more fragrant than the flowers; my heart weeps when even the willow would be silent; my love watches as do never watch floating clouds, nor dewy stars.

Even what of "death, the tomb, sorrow"; a broken heart? He is at rest. *He* knoweth nought of them more. "Only the living know. Only the living."

Oh, my love, my love, would I, too, were above the clouds, and the stars, and the beating storms!

THE END.

www.ingramcontent.com/pod-product-compliance
Lightning Source LLC
Chambersburg PA
CBHW021946160426
43195CB00011B/1243